YOUNG READER'S EDITION

LOOKING LIKE THE ENEMY

MY STORY OF IMPRISONMENT IN JAPANESE-AMERICAN INTERNMENT CAMPS

BY MARY MATSUDA GRUENEWALD

ADAPTED BY MAUREEN R. MICHELSON

NEWSAGE PRESS
Troutdale, Oregon

Young Reader's Edition
LOOKING LIKE THE ENEMY:
My Story of Imprisonment in Japanese-American Internment Camps

Copyright © 2010 Mary Matsuda Gruenewald
Paperback Original ISBN 978-093916558-2

NEWSAGE PRESS
PO Box 607
Troutdale, OR 97060-0607
503-695-2211

website: www.newsagepress.com

Cover Photo: Two children from the Mochida family await evacuation with their parents to a Japanese-American internment camp in Hayward, California on May 8, 1942. The photographer, Dorothea Lange, was an important documentary photographer hired by the U.S. government's War Relocation Authority (WRA) to document the evacuation of Japanese Americans to internment camps. Photo courtesy of Still Picture Records Section, The National Archives. The insert of the Matsuda Family name tag had been attached to one of Mary Matsuda's family suitcases when they were evacuated.

Printed in the United States

The Library of Congress has cataloged the First Edition,
adult memoir, as follows:

Library of Congress Cataloging-in-Publication Data

Gruenewald, Mary Matsuda, 1925-
  Looking like the enemy / by Mary Matsuda Gruenewald.-- 1st ed.
      p. cm.
  Includes bibliographical references.
  ISBN 0-939165-53-8
  1.   Japanese Americans--Evacuation and relocation, 1942-1945. 2. Gruenewald, Mary Matsuda, 1925- 3. Japanese Americans--Biography. I. Title.
  D769.8.A5G78 2005
  940.53'1779635--dc22

                                                                    2005004076

                    1 2 3 4 5 6 7 8 9

DEDICATION

For my parents' generation, the Isseis, whose courage, devotion, and faith in the United States and in their children made it possible for Japanese Americans to triumph over the internment experience.

The Matsuda Family, 1933.

MARY MATSUDA GRUENEWALD COLLECTION

BREAKING
THE SILENCE

One sunny day my brother, Yoneichi, and I sat on a log floating in front of our home at Shawnee Beach on Vashon Island, Washington. I was four years old and Yoneichi was six. On that peaceful day in 1929 we could not know about the difficult future my family would face.

Thirteen years later, World War II broke out and a wave of anti-Japanese prejudice swept across the United States. The government forced my family to leave our secure island home and face a hostile and violent world at war. I did not know that our own country would confine my family in an internment camp simply because we looked like the enemy.

Some seventy-five years later, I gaze long and hard at this photo, recalling my innocence, joy, and security. With what I know now, how I wish I could have held that little girl in the photo and reassured her: "Have faith in your family and the ultimate goodness of people. Especially have faith in yourself to survive the tragic events yet to come. In spite of all the terror, pain, depression, and tears in your future, you will reach a final hopeful conclusion."

Over the years, I have learned faith, hope, and love in a world gone crazy. I have carved out a life marked by reason and patience for myself and for my three children. I also learned the

Mary and Yoneichi.

importance of speaking, telling my story, in the hope that history will not repeat itself.

⊰◉⊱

I wanted to create a young reader's version of my story because I was quite young when this story began. As a teenager, I faced great uncertainty and danger in the United States and worldwide. This story tells how my family lived through that time and learned many important lessons about love and courage. I hope this story offers you hope and inspiration to face whatever challenges may come your way in your own life.

Mary Matsuda Gruenewald
August 2010

MARY MATSUDA GRUENEWALD

Mary Matsuda, 5, and her brother, Yoneichi, 7.

CONTENTS

LOOKING LIKE
THE ENEMY

MARY MATSUDA GRUENEWALD COLLECTION

The Matsuda family's new home on Vashon Island in the winter of 1931.
From left, Yoneichi petting the family dog, Frisky, Papa-san, Mary holding the
family cat, Kitty, and Mama-san. Mary was six years old.

THE DAY MY LIFE CHANGED FOREVER

I will always remember the day my life changed forever.

It was a typical Sunday morning. My brother Yoneichi and I quickly walked through a light rain to get to the local Methodist Church. As usual, we arrived early. We dusted the pews in the small country church and distributed church **hymnals** and bulletins as people arrived.

That December morning my brother and I were happy. We knew all the people in the church, and we always looked forward to singing the familiar hymns and feeling a part of the congregation. The Sunday service was in English so my parents didn't attend. Instead, they would attend services in Japanese, held in their living room whenever a Japanese Methodist minister visited our community.

After church that day, my brother and I wished everyone a good week ahead and left for home. As we walked, I studied the Bible verse I had received and repeated it until I memorized it for next Sunday. That would be my last carefree morning, preoccupied with all the interests and worries of a sixteen-year-old American teenager.

~ ⑥ ~

We had a happy simple life growing up on a rural island called Vashon, just a fifteen-minute ferryboat ride from Seattle, Washington. My life in that beautiful setting was one of innocence and pleasure. I was just one of the island kids. I attended Vashon Grade School with eight grades in one building. Each teacher taught two different classes in the same room.

My parents, Heisuke and Mitsuno Matsuda, had a small berry farm on Vashon Island. We were one of the thirty-seven Japanese-American families living there. My parents worked long days in the berry fields to make a living for their family. They decided to raise their two children on Vashon because they wanted to protect us from the corrupting influences of life in the city.

But nothing could protect us from the events that would soon follow.

◦◉◦

When we got to our house, we cheerfully announced our arrival. My father, whom we always called Papa-san, was sitting at the kitchen table. Normally, Papa-san would have been working outdoors, only returning to the house when lunch was ready. That day, he looked different. His eyes were downcast and he was silent.

Our mother, Mama-san, always greeted us with a smile whenever we came home. But that day, she looked pale as she leaned against the kitchen counter and stared out the window.

"Papa-san, why are you home early?" my brother asked.

When there was no response, Yoneichi's wide smile vanished. His eyes darted back and forth between Papa-san and Mama-san. Then he turned to our mother.

"Mama-san, is something wrong? What's going on?"

I put my things down, suddenly frightened. I had never seen this look on my father's face. I wondered, *Why won't they look at us?*

After a long silence, Papa-san looked up and answered quietly in Japanese. "Mr. Yabu called. Japanese airplanes bombed Pearl Harbor in Hawaii early this morning."

Yoneichi whirled around and snapped on the radio. We didn't have to wait long. The booming voice of an urgent reporter burst out the news of the bomb attack. We listened with horror as he hurriedly spit out information about the heavy losses sustained by the United States Navy.

We all stared at the radio in stunned silence.

This can't be, I thought. *There must be some mistake.*

I didn't want to hear about all the ships that had been hit or that more American servicemen had been killed. But the radio announcer's loud, blaring voice kept interrupting the scheduled programs with more news about the attack.

After awhile, I turned away from the radio and looked at my parents. They understood enough English to grasp the meaning of this announcement. Papa-san's head dropped to his chest, and his shoulders slumped forward. He looked defeated.

Little did we know that Sunday afternoon how much our lives would change, but Papa-san knew enough to be afraid. He realized what could happen if people turned against us because we were Japanese.

Some forty years earlier, shortly after Papa-san's arrival in the United States, my father and several other Japanese men were working in the coalmines in the Alaskan Klondike. One day, a white friend warned my father, "Harry, there's a bunch of guys who don't like you fellows and they are planning to raid your camp tonight. You'd better get out of town right away."

The Japanese men scrambled to gather their things, hurriedly broke up camp, left their jobs, and escaped before the angry mob arrived. Papa-san told me, "I'm grateful for the friendship of some of the *hakujin* (white men). They saved our lives."

When Papa-san told us about this incident, he also described learning first hand about prejudice against people because of the color of their skin or because of the way they looked. He told Yoneichi and me how important it was to develop good relationships with everyone wherever we went.

Now, we realized all those good relationships with our neighbors and business associates would be tested.

Mama-san had been cooking fried chicken for our Sunday meal, but now it was set aside and forgotten in the midst of the unfolding crisis. She was the perfect Japanese wife—obedient and devoted. Ordinarily, Mama-san was lighthearted, gracious, and very practical about life. Today was different.

Now, her eyes filled with tears as she sank into the chair, whispering in Japanese, "This is terribly distressing. What will happen to us?"

Yoneichi and I looked at each other, stunned. We still couldn't believe what was being said on the radio. I thought, *This can't really be happening. Are they insane coming thousands of miles from Japan to attack United States territory? Why did they do this?*

Even though Papa-san had lived in America since 1898, and Mama-san since 1922, they could not become **naturalized citizens.** Many Western states, led by California, had enacted laws that prohibited Japanese arriving from Japan from becoming U.S. citizens. There were also "Anti-alien land laws" that prohibited Japanese from buying and owning land. Similar laws were enacted against the Chinese. These anti-Asian laws were the result of white Americans' fears and prejudices toward Asian immigrants.

We had lived in our home for eleven years, had friendly relationships with our neighbors, and participated in the Vashon community. Still, my parents had no guarantees for their safety because the United States government considered them "aliens." Yoneichi and I had been born in the United States, which made us

American citizens. We were *sure* our citizenship would protect us, but still, we were afraid.

A big knot doubled, then tripled in the pit of my stomach. I was afraid for my family—and for the world. I had a gnawing feeling of guilt because I was Japanese. I didn't want to think about the possibility that American people would consider me as the enemy.

I picked up our cat, Kitty, and sat down on a kitchen chair. Repeatedly, I stroked Kitty's lean silky body and held her close. Our dog, Frisky, sensed something was wrong. He stood nearby and stared at me with his searching gaze. I patted his head and rubbed his ears. In turn, Frisky licked my hand and comforted me as he leaned his body against my legs.

We couldn't stop listening to the radio reports. Yoneichi kept going outdoors, searching the sky for planes. Whenever my brother sat down, his right leg nervously jiggled up and down, unable to contain himself. He kept rubbing his neck as though he had a pain there.

What could my brother possibly be thinking? I wondered.

Yoneichi was a recent high school graduate and was working on the family farm while he thought about his future. Now, his future seemed suspended.

We spent the rest of the day near each other, tense and silent. Radio reports brought more bad news—additional ships destroyed, growing casualties, more disasters wrought. In the end, we would learn that about 2,400 people were killed from the bombing of Pearl Harbor.

In time, we all went outdoors and kept looking at the sky for planes, unable to listen any longer to the radio reports of devastating news. That night, we had very little appetite for dinner and we stayed up later than usual. Each of us spent a restless night.

~ ◉ ~

December 7, 1941, was the day my life changed forever. This was the day the President of the United States, Franklin D. Roosevelt, called "a date which will live in **infamy**." The next day the United States declared war against Japan. On December 11, the United States also declared war against Germany and Italy, two countries that had joined forces with Japan to create the Axis powers. The United States joined other countries called the Allies, in order to fight and stop the Axis powers from invading other countries.

The day Japan bombed Pearl Harbor was also the last day I felt truly American, even though I had been born in the United States. For the rest of my life, I would struggle with the consequences of this day of infamy.

Mitsuno and Heisuke Matsuda, Mary's parents. The photo was taken in 1922 shortly after Heisuke returned to the United States from Japan with his bride.

~CHAPTER TWO~

AM I AMERICAN
OR JAPANESE?

On Monday morning I really did not want to go to school.

I was a junior at Vashon High School and had always enjoyed my classes and being with friends. Now, I felt guilty and ashamed. Japan, my parents' homeland, had done this terrible deed to our United States.

As I walked through the halls from one class to another, every time anyone looked at me, I imagined hatred in their eyes. I assumed they didn't want to have anything to do with me.

Confused and frustrated, I began to cry in one of my classes. Crying seemed to be the only thing I could do. I thought, *I am an American yet I don't look like one. I am Japanese but ashamed that I am.*

The majority of the students in my school were Caucasian, white, but in my grade level there were two Chinese-American students and three Japanese Americans out of a class of seventy-eight. Even though all of my classmates and teachers were kind and behaved the same toward me, everything had changed inside of me. It was clear all the students shared my fear of the future and the shock of the sudden turn of events.

Not one person did anything to single me out or blame me. A friend came up and linked her arm with mine as we walked together to English class. My classmates offered their silent support, and I was grateful, but now I felt like an outsider. Ever since the third grade, when one of the mean white kids called me a "Jap," I knew I was different. But still, we got along pretty well. Only now, things were not the same.

All the years my family lived on Vashon Island, our parents had stressed the importance of being good citizens of the community and nation. "America is made up of people from all walks of life from many countries of the world," they declared. "The equality of all of the people, and tolerance, are keys to living peacefully together."

My parents had taught us to control our emotions, and to be calm, brave, and respectful of authority. But on that Monday after Pearl Harbor, I felt incredible tension building inside of me. Afraid and helpless, I couldn't do the thing that I most wanted—to change things back to the way they were.

⊰◉⊱

That evening as we ate dinner we listened to radio reports. The U.S. government's Office of Civil Defense made an important announcement: "Beginning this evening at 7:00, all citizens in the Puget Sound area are required to implement a complete, dusk-to-dawn, visual blackout to prevent an attack on our defense industries."

The blackout was to last every night until further notice. Everybody had to obey this government order. My family briefly discussed what we had to do to be sure no light was visible outside of our home.

Mama-san got up from the table and said to me, "Mary-san, help me gather up some blankets to cover our windows. We'll have to bring out the old kerosene lamps, too."

Yoneichi got a stepladder and helped drape the blankets over every window. If there were enemy airplanes flying over the West Coast, the blackout would keep the enemy from seeing lights and possibly bombing important areas of California, Oregon, and Washington.

"I wonder what will happen next," Yoneichi said. "You don't suppose more Japanese planes will come over and bomb us here, do you?"

After a few moments, he added, "And what about us? Surely it will make a difference because we have been good citizens in our community. Mary and I are Americans, not Japanese. Won't that make a difference?"

His questions trailed off. No one could answer them.

A few days later, when I was in the living room doing my homework, I overheard my parents talking. Papa-san said with a worried tone, "I wish Japan hadn't attacked Pearl Harbor. Our lives will certainly become more difficult."

"Yes, I'm afraid they will," Mama-san replied, distressed. "It's hard to tell who will still be our friends and who will turn against us. I hope our neighbors will still be friendly."

Papa-san added, "Yes, and I think it is important for us to cooperate with the civil defense efforts. We'll do whatever we can to show that we are good citizens in spite of everything."

My parents continued talking in Japanese in hushed voices as if to protect Yoneichi and me.

⊰◉⊱

In the fall of 1941, before the bombing of Pearl Harbor, there was no way we could have known how close the United States was to entering World War II. We never thought a small nation like Japan would attempt to attack a world power like the United States.

We also didn't know that the U.S. government had conducted a study a decade earlier that examined the loyalty of Japanese Americans living on the West Coast and Hawaii. The U.S. government study found that "there is no Japanese problem." The government kept this information secret, never telling the public prior to World War II, during the war years, or in the years shortly thereafter.

Of course, I knew nothing about the worldwide problems erupting and involving almost every major country around the world. In 1941, I was sixteen years old, happy with my family, my school, and my life. All during my childhood I had believed that I was "one of the group" in America—both Japanese and American. It was wonderful.

One of my first-grade classmates on Vashon Island, whose family spoke only Japanese at home, had a different experience. Occasionally, the teacher left the classroom for a minute, leaving the children on their honor. One of the boys shot spit wads around the room, causing problems. When the teacher returned and wanted to know who was the troublemaker, the boy pointed to my friend as the offender. The teacher disciplined my friend with many swats on the hand with a wooden ruler. My friend did not know how to defend himself from the teacher or from the offending classmate until much later.

When Yoneichi started school, he had a difficult time understanding his teachers because we only spoke Japanese at home. He almost flunked the first grade, but with additional tutoring in English, Yoneichi caught on quickly and eventually graduated as the student ranking second highest academically in his high school class. Because Yoneichi was two years ahead of me, I learned English from him and I had a much easier time starting school.

⊰❀⊱

For several weeks, high school proceeded as though things were unchanged, even though my world felt turned upside down. My classmates were busy planning an elaborate junior prom, but this did not interest me. Instead, I was struggling to understand what was happening and the implications for my family's future.

I attended classes, but I had a hard time concentrating. In English III, we studied poetry and that caught my attention. I began collecting poems, made my own poetry book, and included illustrations. The poems took me outside myself, comforting me in a way that nothing else could. A poem by Rudyard Kipling **foreshadowed** what was in store for my family and other Japanese Americans.

IF

If you can keep your head when all about you
Are losing theirs and blaming it on you;
If you can trust yourself when all men doubt you,
But make allowance for their doubting too:
If you can wait and not be tired by waiting,
Or being lied about, don't deal in lies,
Or being hated don't give way to hating,
And yet don't look too good, nor talk too wise...

After bombing Pearl Harbor, the Japanese forces invaded Guam, Hong Kong, Manila, and Singapore. The United States was fighting Japan in what was called the "Asia-Pacific War" or "Pacific War," which was part of World War II. The Asia-Pacific War took place in the Pacific Ocean, its islands, and countries in the Far East. In addition, The United States and the Allied Forces (mainly Great Britain, France, and the Soviet Union) were fighting Germany, Italy, and other Axis countries in Europe. The Axis forces had brutally invaded and occupied many European countries, including Poland, Austria, France, Norway, and Denmark, among others.

In the United States, people were afraid of a Japanese invasion. People living in the West Coast states of California, Oregon, and Washington felt especially vulnerable and fearful of Japan's aggression because Japan had bombed Pearl Harbor. In addition, Japan had already invaded China, Mongolia, and European colonies in Asia.

The Asia-Pacific War brought increased attention to the Japanese and Japanese Americans living in Hawaii and on the West Coast. Many people in the United States began to blame Japanese Americans as **conspirator**s responsible for the attack on Pearl Harbor.

There were false stories in local newspapers and on radio broadcasts reporting that Japanese in Hawaii who supported Japan's attack had cut arrows into the cane fields, directing Japanese planes to bomb Pearl Harbor. There were reports of Japanese Americans on the West Coast plotting against the U.S. government.

Although these rumors were never proven as true, the Western Defense Commander for the U.S. government, General John L. DeWitt, insisted "no proof of **sabotage** was indeed proof that sabotage was imminent." This statement did not make any sense, but sadly, people accepted it as the truth. Even California's Attorney General, Earl Warren, who was the main legal advisor to the state's government, agreed with and supported DeWitt's opinion of the Japanese-American threat.

⊰◎⊱

As the anti-Japanese **propaganda** spread throughout the West Coast and the United States, I began to withdraw more and more. I started to drop my eyes whenever anyone approached me. I was never much of a talker, and now I spoke even less in those months following the bombing of Pearl Harbor.

My parents had already experienced **discrimination**, so they were not surprised at the severe distortion of Japanese Americans in the press and elsewhere. However, this was the first time I had really experienced discrimination and I could not believe nor accept what was happening. I also knew the negative claims against Japanese Americans were false. I started to blame myself for being Japanese.

Popular magazines like *Time* portrayed cartoons of Japanese soldiers with yellow skin and squinty, slanted eyes. They had huge, white buckteeth framed by a sneering grin. The cartoons portrayed the Japanese soldiers with tiny button noses, high prominent cheekbones, and large pointed heads under little ugly military caps. These cartoons made the Japanese soldiers look like crazed monkeys or insane evil men.

Along with the cartoons, *Time* magazine published an article, "How to Tell Your Friends From the Japs." It discussed how difficult it was to tell the difference between Chinese and Japanese people. Some examples were that Chinese are taller and slimmer, not as hairy, and their facial expressions are more peaceful, kindly, and open. In Washington, D.C., a newspaper journalist wore a large badge on his lapel that said, "Chinese Reporter— NOT Japanese—please." These articles made it clear that it was okay to be friends with the Chinese, but not the Japanese.

I hated what I heard and read, but I couldn't help but pay atten-

OUR CARELESSNESS
Their Secret Weapon

PREVENT FOREST FIRES

U. S. DEPT. OF AGRICULTURE   STATE
FOREST SERVICE   FOREST SERVICE

THE NATIONAL ARCHIVES

A U.S. government poster used war ***propaganda*** *to encourage people to prevent forest fires. The cartoon image of Japan's Emperor Hirohito portrays an ugly racist view of all Japanese. These kind of images were common during World War II. The image of Adolf Hitler, the leader of Nazi Germany, is also in this poster.*

tion to newspaper and magazine stories, and radio broadcasts. I wondered, *Is that how people see me?* I wished I had never been born.

I wanted to run away and hide but there was no place to go. There was no way I could change my skin color, my eyes, my straight black hair, or my name. I was ashamed of myself and started to hate myself. Yet, that's the way it was—I looked like the enemy.

I began to have frequent stomach pains. Food didn't taste good even though Mama-san's cooking was always delicious. I began having nightmares with a constant theme of trying to run, but my legs wouldn't work right. In some nightmares, I was running down stairs and falling but never hitting bottom. Many nights I would wake up in a cold sweat, my heart pounding, gasping for breath.

Am I Japanese? Or am I American? This became the defining question I asked myself daily.

From my earliest memories, I had been both. I grew up playing hopscotch and jacks, while also learning *kendo*, a Japanese martial art using bamboo sticks for swords. I studied U.S. history at school and Japanese on Saturday. For breakfast, I ate scrambled eggs and *mochi*, a Japanese rice cake. Dinner could include fried chicken and sushi.

I always felt that I was Japanese American and I belonged in America. I was part of the group called "Americans." Before December 7, 1941, it never occurred to me that I was not.

~CHAPTER THREE~

BEING JAPANESE
IN AMERICA

The Japanese who came to America were looking for a better life.

In many ways, they were just like every other group of people who came to this country. Many came to escape problems in their homeland, such as famine, religious persecution, war, or a particular way of life that was not satisfying. Others, like my parents, came because they were drawn to the promise of opportunities and an exciting new life in America.

The problems facing newly arrived Japanese as well as other immigrants were overwhelming. Most immigrants had to learn a new language in a foreign land. How do you eat when you can't find the foods you are familiar with and only see strange foods? What do you do if you can't even ask questions about the food that is available? How do you get a job when you can't speak the same language as your boss or customers? How do you work and support yourself and your family?

In order to survive in a different setting, many immigrant groups established cultural centers, such as Japantown, Little Italy, or Chinatown. These cultural communities made it easier for immigrants to survive financially and socially. However, these centers also isolated the immigrant population from neighbors outside of their cultural group.

In all immigrant populations, the parents worked hard to establish a firm foothold in the new country. My parents were first generation Japanese Americans and they were called *Isseis*. They were like most hardworking immigrants, sacrificing their own needs so their family could have a future in America.

To a large degree, my parents continued with old country customs, spoke traditional Japanese, ate Japanese food, and celebrated Japanese holidays. Before 1941, the Japanese in America were culturally isolated, a people without a future.

Yoneichi and I were second generation Japanese Americans and we were called *Niseis*. We were U.S. citizens and we spoke English well. Still, we could not expect professional careers.

Niseis had trouble finding jobs outside of the Japanese-American community. Most took low-paying jobs far below their capabilities, working in Japantowns up and down the West Coast, or in their parents' businesses. My parents ran their own farm and berry business. It looked as if their future in America

was secure. They had not imagined the trouble that awaited them.

~ ⑥ ~

Like many children of immigrants, Yoneichi and I often had to be translators for our parents. When interacting with the larger community, we would translate from Japanese to English, and then from English to Japanese. As the second generation, we *Niseis* became more American through our

Vashon Methodist Church school activities, friendships with non-Japanese students, and exposure to the radio and newspapers. (However there was no television when I was growing up.)

One Sunday when I was in First Grade, shortly after we moved into our new house, Papa-san took Yoneichi and me by the hand and walked us toward the town of Vashon. The first church we came to looked inviting, so he dropped us off. We met the minister and Sunday school staff and began attending the Methodist church every Sunday.

Yoneichi and I listened to the radio every evening in our home. Our first radio was a gift from an old neighbor who gave it to Yoneichi when he was six years old in 1929. My parents were not too interested in the radio, especially since all of the broadcasts were in English. But it immediately became Yoneichi's favorite toy, and he listened to the radio every night with headphones. Often, he would act out what he heard. Because only one person could listen at a time, I had to beg for my turn to listen.

One night when we were supposed to be asleep, a week or so after we got the radio, Yoneichi was listening to a radio program. I kept waving my hands in front of his eyes, nagging him to let me listen. He kept saying, "Wait a minute, just wait another minute, okay?"

I continued to insist with the persistence of a four year old. Then all of a sudden, Yoneichi grabbed the headphones from his head and in one swift movement clamped them over my ears. In that moment, my young mind expanded to unimagined worlds.

"CHANDU the Magician." BONG!

Then a deep, menacing, male voice barked, "Twelve o'clock at midnight! Even walls have ears!"

An earsplitting, scary laugh cackled in my head. I pulled the headphones off and plunged under the covers crying hysterically. Mama-san came rushing in and gave us heck for still being awake and making so much noise.

By the time I was ten, the radio was like another member of the family. I liked to listen to radio shows like Jack Benny

A Japanese family digging for clams on Puget Sound. Mary and her family often dug for clams on Vashon Island shores.

and Amos 'N' Andy. I also read the Sunday funnies with Flash Gordon, Dick Tracy, and Little Orphan Annie. One time I persuaded Papa-san to buy a rich chocolate drink, Ovaltine, because it was advertised on the Little Orphan Annie radio program. I wanted to mail the Ovaltine's inside seal for a ring to decode secret messages given during the show. It was fun comparing the messages with my classmates. In many ways, Yoneichi and I were typical American kids.

Throughout childhood and our teen years, Yoneichi and I found ourselves caught between the traditions of our parents and the influences of our American friends. As the obedient daughter, I never complained, but I longed to go with my friends to buy candy and ice cream, or wear makeup, or go to movies and dances. When the carnival came to Vashon with the merry-go-round, Ferris wheel, and other kids' rides, we did not go. I could hear the carousel music from our house, and I wished I could go. I never asked because I knew my parents would frown upon such a suggestion. They would have considered the carnival foolish.

While my parents wanted us to adapt to some American ways, they were also sure about the importance of Japanese values. Traditional Japanese culture emphasizes family and group-centered activities. Unlike the dominant American culture, which emphasizes individuality first, in Japanese families children are reminded continuously how their behavior is a reflection on the whole family.

꒰◉꒱

Several important concepts are essential in a traditional Japanese family, and they were the foundation of our family life on Vashon. The Japanese word, *"on,"* is an expression for a powerful sense of loyalty, respect, and gratitude toward others, especially one's parents. Our *on* for one another was expressed daily through our family duties and through respectful verbal communication.

Mama-san was always the first to get up in the morning and the last to go to bed at night. She and Papa-san showed complete devotion to one another, and worked hard for our benefit. Before starting every meal, Yoneichi and I would always say, *"Itadaki masu"* to Mama-san in a respectful tone of voice with a slight nod of the head. This means, "I gratefully receive this meal you have prepared for us."

Mama-san's traditional response would be, *"Dozo,"* (Please, by all means.) or *"Itadaki masho."* (Let's eat!) She, too, would look at us and respond with a smile and a slight nod of her head.

After each meal we would say, *"Gochiso sama deshita."* (It was very delicious.) This was a compliment of respect and appreciation going deeper than the flavor of the meal.

Every time we left home for any reason, we would always say to our folks, *"It-te kimasu...."* (I am going to....) We would include where we were going.

Their response was always, *"It-te irashai."* (Please be on your way.) Our greeting when we returned home was, *"Tadaima kaeri-mashita."* (I have just returned home.)

In the spirit of *on,* we would never think of doing things without going through these short but respectful rituals with our parents. It was our way of maintaining closeness in our family. Some of my non-Japanese friends said our conversations sounded so formal, and indeed they may have been.

Yoneichi and I also learned *giri,* which means a sense of duty, obligation, and loyalty to one's family or group. A common statement Papa-san and Mama-san offered to Yoneichi and me in the spirit of *giri* was, "You will always want to conduct yourself properly because you don't want to bring *haji* (shame) on our family and the other Japanese families on Vashon Island."

Throughout my childhood my parents reminded me to be polite, respect others, study hard, and get the best grades possible. Hand-in-hand with this Japanese value was another Japanese principle, *enryo,* which implies restraint, modesty, and humility in our daily actions. We were never to brag or to take excessive credit for anything.

Although my parents never used the word "love," in Japanese or in English, they clearly communicated it. Their love was in their eyes and their smiles whenever they spoke to us. Papa-san wasn't as verbal as Mama-san, yet he had his own ways of letting us know how much he cherished us.

Whenever he had to travel to Seattle for business, Papa-san brought each of us our favorite foods. I got wonderful fruits, such as persimmons, pomegranates, watermelon, and peaches. Yoneichi got cakes, pies, cookies and candy. Papa-san found special Japanese goodies for Mama-san. My father was like a Japanese Santa, joyfully bringing home overstuffed bags with gifts, carrying them long distances on the bus.

The Japanese children on Vashon all attended Japanese language school every Saturday during the regular school year. Most of us students protested silently against the parental requirement that we learn to read and write Japanese, especially all day on Saturday.

The Japanese kids in Seattle had to attend Japanese language school five days a week after their regular school day.

Yoneichi was the first-born and male, so he felt an obligation to learn Japanese and study hard to master the language. I felt compelled to learn, too, but I didn't study as hard as Yoneichi. Years later, the Japanese I learned would be important because I could write to my parents in Japanese.

Mary (right) with Mama-san and a friend on Vashon, Michi Nakamichi. In this photo Mary was 16 years old, and her life was still carefree and happy. Soon, her world would be turned upside down.

Leisure time within our family was spent doing light tasks around the property. We planted or weeded flowerbeds, pruned fruit trees, tended beehives, experimented with **grafting** apples on a common tree, and tried our hand at growing rhododendron plants. We were successful with almost all of them except the rhododendron plants.

During the winter months, Mama-san made futons, a traditional Japanese mattress made with cotton batting covered with colorful cotton covers. She and I also made jams and jellies, pickles, cookies, and pies. We liked to experiment making different kinds of food to the delight of the family.

Each year, a few days before January 1, eight to ten Japanese families on Vashon would come to our home to make *mochi*, which is steamed rice pounded and formed into cakes. On New Year's Eve, we always stayed up until midnight to wish each other a Happy New Year. We ate a special hot dish of sweet dark beans and *mochi* soup.

The next day the Japanese men and boys would visit each Japanese household on Vashon to eat *sushi, tempura,* and other delicacies, and give the women and girls in each home their greeting. This ritual gave everyone in our community a chance to visit with each other during the dark winter months.

While I am sure that the Japanese "city kids" had somewhat different traditions than we did on Vashon, those Japanese traditions were just as important in maintaining a sense of community.

One important difference between Japanese living in rural America and Japanese living in cities was the degree to which families **assimilated** into the larger American culture. In the city, it was possible for Japanese-American families to stick with their own groups and limit interaction with the larger American society. However, Japanese families on Vashon were scattered throughout the island, so we had a more integrated Americanized lifestyle.

As a carefree teenager about to be thrown into the chaos and devastation of World War II, I had no idea how these Japanese values would help my family and me. In time, these values would give us the strength to endure.

The events about to unfold could have destroyed my family and many other Japanese-American families. Instead, the wisdom of our heritage enabled us to weather the storm of internment camps and emerge stronger.

BURNING OUR
JAPANESE TREASURES

Finally, we found out we would have to leave our home.

President Franklin Delano Roosevelt issued Executive Order 9066 on February 19, 1942, two-and-a-half months after the bombing of Pearl Harbor. This presidential order directed the Secretary of War to begin the mass evacuation of Japanese residents from the Washington, Oregon, and California coasts. The President issued this order in spite of information collected for years by naval intelligence and the FBI documenting that Japanese living in the United States were *not* a threat.

I read the newspaper stories with a mixture of dread and relief, finally getting answers to questions I had dared not ask. Unfortunately, for every question that was answered there were ten new questions to be asked.

After dinner that evening the four of us sat around the dinner table to discuss the evacuation order.

"There are a lot of questions that will have to be answered," Papa-san said. "For instance, when will we have to leave? How can we care for our property while we're away?"

"And where will we be going?" Mama-san asked. "How long will we be gone?"

At school, my teachers were kind and understanding. They called on me in class only when I raised my hand. One day after Latin class, my teacher, Mrs. Keyes, pulled me aside and said, "Mary, I've been wanting to ask you how you're doing these days. This must be a terrible time for you and your family. Is there anything I can do for you?"

"Thanks, Mrs. Keyes, you're already doing what I need the most, just treating me normally. Just keep doing what you've been doing."

My family still clung to our belief that perhaps the evacuation orders might spare Yoneichi and me because we were American citizens.

One evening after dinner, Yoneichi said to me, "According to the newspaper, if there is an evacuation order, it would apply only to *Isseis* (first generation) and the *Kibeis* (those born in the U.S., educated in Japan, and returned to the U.S. again). That would mean you and I would stay here with other U.S. born Japanese, and our parents would be taken somewhere else."

Yoneichi put the paper down angrily. "There's no way we can run the farm and take care of the folks when they get sent away to some godforsaken place. I don't like that at all."

"Me neither," I replied. "How are they going to get along without us to help them understand what will probably be told to them in English? That isn't the way we do things in our family."

⊰◉⊱

One Saturday morning in late February, Mama-san received an alarming phone call from Mrs. Yamamoto on nearby Bainbridge Island. She was shouting so loud through the phone that I could hear her as her words tumbled into a stream of sentences.

"Two men from the FBI were here this morning to search our place," Mrs. Yamamoto began. "And do you know what those men did? One of them looked all around the yard before coming inside. They asked all kinds of questions about guns and short wave radios, all sorts of things. They took out some of our books, flipped through them, and asked what they were about. Then they ran their hands through our rice bin, our sugar, and rummaged through most of our kitchen and bedroom drawers and closets. It was awful, just awful. I felt like a common thief."

Mama-san tried to respond but Mrs. Yamamoto continued. "At Fuji's home, they took some books on radios, but over at Tadashi's house they found some dynamite. They sure asked lots of questions about what he was going to use it for. Tadashi told them that he used it years ago to clear his land and had forgotten that he had any left. I don't know if they believed him or not. They took it away with them anyway. You folks on Vashon Island are probably going to be next."

In a lowered voice, Mrs. Yamamoto warned Mama-san, "Get rid of *anything* that can tie you too closely to Japan. That's what they're looking for—and if they find anything, they might take your husband and send him off somewhere far away, or some other terrible thing."

We were shaken by the call but grateful for the warning. Immediately, we started looking at everything in our home. We went through every drawer, closet, cupboard, and shelf looking frantically at everything that could possibly threaten our future.

Papa-san and Yoneichi went through the barn and woodshed, too. We gathered all our special things that reminded us of Japan and put them together in several boxes, ready to burn after dark. We had to get rid of these things because the risk of being labeled even faintly "disloyal" was just too great.

That evening after dusk while we still had our work clothes on, we brought out the boxes with all of our treasures. Papa-san took out all the special Japanese phonograph records and placed them together on one side of the dining room table. Next to that, Mama-san placed all the family photos from both sides of their families in Japan.

Then she brought out our beautiful Japanese dolls that we would display on special Japanese holidays like *Hina Matsuri,* also called "Doll Festival" or "Girls Day" on March 3, and *Tango No Sekku,* also called "Boys Day" on May 5. We were afraid the FBI agents would see the Japanese dolls as symbols of loyalty to Japan.

Finally, Mama-san reached into the bottom of the last box and brought out her prized books of Japanese classic literature and Japanese history, along with magazines, books of fairy tales, and children's books.

We stood in front of the table looking at all of our Japanese treasures. Papa-san took a deep breath and said, "This is it. Let's get this difficult task done."

He picked up the first phonograph record, read the label, and said to Mama-san, "This one, '*Sakura,*' is my favorite."

He handed the record to Mama-san, who also read the label. With teary eyes she broke it into small pieces, then stepped over to the stove and slipped it into the flames. They looked at each record and took turns breaking them, silently feeding their beloved music into the fire until every record was destroyed.

Our photographs of relatives in Japan came next. Together, Mama-san and Papa-san looked at each picture with tired and sad eyes, and talked about each person. Then they tossed the family photos into the burning stove, one by one, imploring each image as it burned,

"*Gomen nasai ne.*" (Forgive me for what I am doing.)

"*Gomen nasai ne.*"

With increasingly heavy hearts, we turned our attention to our Japanese dolls of the emperor and empress sitting in regal splendor with several ladies in waiting and samurai warriors. Each of us looked at the dolls for a long time, noticing how delicate and perfect they were in every detail.

Heaving a big sigh, Yoneichi picked up a samurai warrior doll and studied it carefully. He gently touched the warrior's clothes, the sword by his side, and hair. Then he looked at Papa-san and Mama-san. At their nod, Yoneichi walked over to the stove and flung the warrior into the flames. He quickly bowed his head and turned away from us.

Then Papa-san looked at me and nodded for me to take my turn. Reluctantly, I looked at the remaining dolls to see which one I should take. I could scarcely breathe as I carefully picked up one of the ladies in waiting. She was my favorite. Her kimono was a shim-

RAY GRUENEWALD

This Japanese doll is similar to the dolls Mary and her family burned in the fire. When Mary was 80 years old, she bought the Japanese doll in this photo to replace the beloved doll from her childhood.

mering delicate light pink. Her face was calm and composed—nothing like what I was feeling. I slipped the doll behind my back and quickly grasped another lady in waiting. Moving to the front of the stove, I flung the second one into the roaring fire. I couldn't bear to watch the hungry flames consume the beautiful doll.

As each of us took turns throwing the dolls into the burning fire, I looked away but I could still hear the roar of the flames feeding on our precious possessions. Papa-san's jaws were set and a deep crease remained between his eyebrows. He flung the emperor doll into the bright fire. Mama-san kept wiping the tears away with the edge of her apron as she did the same with the empress doll.

Finally, it was time for me to part with my favorite doll. Slowly, I walked to the front of the stove, gave my doll one final squeeze, then flung her into the inferno that seared my heart like some fierce drag-on destroying all that I loved. With tears streaming down my face, I turned away. I could feel the heat and hear the roar of the flames as they consumed my doll's delicate body in a matter of seconds.

I thought about the last time Mama-san carefully set up the doll display for us. She said, "These are very special dolls just like you and your brother are so special to us."

Now it was time to turn our attention to Mama-san's Japanese books. They had been so important to us. When she came to our favorite fairy tale of Momotaro, the Peach Boy, I asked her, "Mama-san, would you read it to us for the last time, please?"

And she did as Yoneichi and I sat nearby, listening.

Momotaro grew up to become an extraordinary soldier who left his parents to fight a band of devils who were stealing from people in the countryside. He took a large dog, a monkey, and a pheasant to help him conquer the devils, free the prisoners, and return the things that had been stolen from the people. Momotaro was a hero and the valuables he brought back allowed his parents to live in peace and comfort for the rest of their lives.

After this fifteen-minute story, Mama-san closed the book and placed her hand on top of it. Yoneichi remarked wistfully, "That is such a great fairy tale. I wish we could have such a wonderful thing to look forward to."

Little did we know at the time that Yoneichi would, in fact, go with many other young Japanese-American men, just like Momotaro. He would go off to fight for democracy and freedom for all of us.

Mama-san sadly took the book over to the stove and forced herself to throw the exquisitely illustrated book into the fire. The only Japanese book we didn't burn was the Bible. That fateful day we burned all of our Japanese treasures in the oil burning stove in the living room.

The next day, I saw Yoneichi dig a deep hole in the ground on the side of our house. "Yoneichi, what are you doing?" I asked.

"I've spent a lot of time on this story that I wrote in Japanese," he explained. "If I put it into this can and bury it, I hope I can save it."

When Yoneichi was done hiding his Japanese story like a buried treasure, we turned our attention to the house and yard to make everything look untouched and normal just in case the FBI questioned us. We were also careful not to disturb the cobwebs in the corners of each room or the dust on the picture frames. We didn't want it to look as if we had hidden anything.

～⊙～

Years later, I realized how hasty we were in destroying our Japanese mementos, but at that time we were afraid. We thought if we destroyed those things that represented some of our most precious Japanese cultural gems, then Papa-san wouldn't be taken away from us. Perhaps we wouldn't be evacuated either. In the end, it would make no difference to the government authorities.

One evening when I was doing the dinner dishes, I noticed that a very beautiful Japanese vase was not in its usual place. The set of silverware was gone, too. I didn't need to ask to understand that Mama-san had quietly given away her prized possessions to neighbors she knew would value them.

Later, I had a shocking thought as I caught a glimpse of myself in the mirror. *After all we had done to protect ourselves, nothing had changed.* My hair was still coarse, straight, and black. My skin was yellow, and my eyes were small and slanted.

We tried to erase our Japanese history by destroying all those precious things, but we couldn't escape from the way we looked. Nothing could change that. And in the end, all that mattered to the United States government was what we looked like.

THE FBI SEARCHES OUR HOUSE

A shiny black car pulled slowly into our driveway.

I watched from the kitchen window, frozen. I had been washing the breakfast dishes before going to the fields to work with my family.

Oh, oh. This doesn't look good! I thought.

Two tall, clean-shaven, grim-faced white men dressed in black suits got out. They came to the back door and asked, "Is this the residence of Heisuke Matsuda?"

Gripping the door handle to keep my hand from shaking, I answered, "It is."

Each man revealed his badge and said, "We're from the FBI. We would like to talk with him. Is he at home?"

Trying to keep my voice calm, I said, "My father and the rest of the family are out in the field. I will go out there and have them come home."

My breathing quickened at the thought of why the FBI agents were here. Just a few weeks earlier we had burned all of our Japanese treasures, just in case this day would come. The FBI had already taken away the president of our Japanese association on Vashon shortly after the bombing of Pearl Harbor. Now, I worried, *Are they here for my father, too?*

Papa-san had been the secretary of the association for years, and I was almost certain they had come to take him away. I quickly erased the image of the big arm of the United States government reaching all the way from Washington D.C. and grabbing Papa-san away from us.

The agents began to look around the yard and I briefly saw one of them kneel down to peer into the crawl space under the house. A wave of **nausea** settled over me as I headed toward the fields.

My legs felt weak and wobbly from the weight of what I had to tell my family. The sun was out but it felt cold and chilly. I wanted to run and blurt the news quickly to get it over with, but at the same time, I just wanted to sit down at the edge of the field and not tell them anything at all.

I thought, *Perhaps I could yell and scream and wake myself up from this bad dream.* But it was no dream.

I had to get Papa-san right away. When I finally forced myself out to the field where everyone was hoeing, my mouth felt full of cotton. "Papa-san, two men from the FBI have come to the house, and they want to talk with you."

No one moved. No one said a thing for a long time. They had the pained look of being "caught." Papa-san heaved a big sigh and said, "It looks like the time has finally come. Mama-san, you stay here. Yoneichi-san and I will go to the house with Mary-san."

Mama-san and I exchanged fearful glances.

As the three of us returned to the house, I thought about a lot of things: *Have they come to take Papa-san away from us? How will we get along without him? Will they take our farm, too?*

Now, these two strangers from the FBI were here to search our home. As I led them through the utility room into the familiar, homey kitchen, my heart pounded so hard I was afraid the agents could hear it. Mama-san had decorated the kitchen in white and soft lime-green. The kitchen window, framed in white cottage curtains, looked out onto the lawn, which was surrounded by a short evergreen hedge, flowers, and a camellia bush ready to bloom.

Across from the wood stove were our kitchen table and four chairs. This was our family's daily gathering spot for meals and family conversations. The kitchen was the heart of our home.

The men stood in the middle of the kitchen. I was to their right, Yoneichi to their left, and Papa-san stood behind us. The men slowly looked at everything from one side of the room to the other, up above at the ceiling, and along the linoleum-lined floor below. As they asked us to open specific drawers or cupboards, we did so promptly. They began taking notes.

One of the men said to me, "Would you pull out that drawer please?" indicating the one to the right of the sink.

Holding my breath, I did as he asked. He pointed to a well-worn, little book lying there and asked, "What is that book?"

I opened it and showed it to him, saying, "This is my parents' New Testament in Japanese. They read from it often. We are Methodists." I thought this fact might make us seem less foreign. He nodded. I put it back and closed the drawer.

Next, he asked to look in the broom closet. I had butterflies in my stomach as I saw them looking at Yoneichi's .22 caliber rifle. He used it to shoot pellets at the crows that raided our strawberries in the springtime. They didn't say a word but they wrote something in their notebook.

We proceeded into the living room. The agents saw our matching sofa and chair, the oil burning stove over to the right, my piano to the left, and a small table beside it with a record player on top. The dining room table occupied the center of the room. I held my hands tightly together as I saw them taking special note of the console radio standing against the wall.

"Can you get Japanese broadcasts through that?" one of the agents asked.

Yoneichi replied, "We can occasionally when weather conditions are clear, but most of the time there is so much static that the folks can't understand most of it."

"What capabilities do you have for sending messages to Japan?" the same agent asked.

"None," answered Yoneichi. "We don't have any equipment to do that."

Their eyes scanned everything in my parents' bedroom and closet, the bathroom, and the spare bedroom and closet on the main floor. There was nothing that caught their attention. When we went upstairs to Yoneichi's and my bedrooms, their big shoes clomped up the wooden stairs behind me. When they looked in my room, nothing interested them.

The agents opened the little doors off each room that led to the unfinished crawl spaces in the attic. They took their time looking all around with their flashlights. There was nothing up there except a few old pictures of movie stars that I had clipped and saved in a flat box. When the agents were done searching the house, they seemed satisfied. However, they did take away two items: my brother's .22 caliber rifle and the large console radio.

When the agents finally left, I put my hand on Papa-san's shoulder and gave him a squeeze. Tears streaked my cheeks. A broad smile of relief crossed Papa-san's face bringing color back to his cheeks. We hurried out to the field to share the good news with Mama-san who had been waiting anxiously. She relaxed when she saw our faces.

I, too, was relieved, thinking, *They didn't take my father away.*

U.S. soldier posting a Civilian Exclusion Order.

LEAVING OUR HOME

More government orders restricted our lives and chipped away at many of our freedoms.

In mid-March, the government ordered a curfew that required all Japanese on the West Coast to stay in their homes from 8 p.m. to 6 a.m. This curfew was probably easier for us on the farm than for Japanese who lived in the city or owned businesses such as restaurants and hotels. They depended on customers and needed to be open for business.

In addition, the U.S. government restricted Japanese Americans to travel no more than fifteen miles from their homes. This meant we could not get off the island for any reason.

The government had ordered all Japanese-American bank accounts to be frozen for several weeks right after Pearl Harbor. That meant we couldn't get our money from the bank. Eventually, we were allowed to withdraw up to $100 per month to cover our expenses.

These increasing government restrictions created a lot of fear among Japanese Americans about what would happen to us. Whenever I went out to the main highway to get our mail, I cautiously looked both ways before I dared to step out to the mailbox and grab the mail. Then I would run home. Even when I went to church on Sundays, I searched everyone's faces fearfully—not even sure what I was afraid of, but still watching carefully.

✎◎✎

On March 30, 1942, the government issued its first official order for the evacuation of Japanese Americans from Washington State's Puget Sound area.. When we learned each person would be allowed to carry only two suitcases of belongings, we ordered eight large suitcases through the Sears & Roebuck catalogue.

One night, our family huddled around the kitchen table and tried to plan what we should take. We decided each of us would take one pair of sheets, a pillowcase, and one blanket. Clothes included one heavy winter overcoat, several sweaters, two blouses or shirts, two pair of slacks or skirts, a week's worth of socks and underwear, one pair of shoes, and a flannel nightgown or pajamas.

In addition to personal toilet articles, we would include silverware, a cup, and a plate. I wanted to take my English Bible and a small radio.

As we packed, questions swirled in my head: *Will this be enough? How long will we be gone? What kind of weather will we have to live through? Will there be anything to buy if we don't have the right things? Will we have enough money to buy things if we need them?*

There were many questions but no answers.

While we anxiously waited for the government's order to evacuate, we kept working the farm. There was always weeding, planting, replacing sickly strawberry plants with healthy ones, and fertilizing to ensure healthy fruit in the coming months. Digging and planting and tending to our berry crop kept us busy. Hard work helped us sleep better at night and not worry too much. Perhaps this was our way to keep believing in the future even though great uncertainty surrounded us.

On the evening of May 8, Papa-san got a phone call. As he listened, he turned and stared at Mama-san for a few moments, then turned away.

When he hung up the phone, he turned to us and said, "That was Hiroshi Morita. He said we have to leave in eight days." The three of us stared at Papa-san, speechless, his words echoing in the long silence that followed.

Suddenly, my future had shrunk to eight precious days. After that, there was only the unknown. For the rest of the evening I stayed close to my family as we tried to figure out what needed to be done.

The next day, Yoneichi walked the half-mile to see the government's official order nailed to a telephone pole near Hiroshi's house.

Government instructions listed what each evacuee must carry, including bedding, toilet articles, extra clothing, plates, bowls, silverware, cups, and essential personal items. No pets of any kind would be permitted. Government storage at the sole risk of the owner was available if the belongings were properly marked.

Yoneichi came home and told us what he saw. "You and I, Mary, are called 'non-alien.' They don't call us citizens, which is what we are!"

He frowned and flung himself in the nearby chair. It did not matter that Yoneichi and I, by **birthright**, were U.S. citizens. In one fell swoop, the government robbed us of our rights. Now, because of our Japanese heritage, we were the "non-aliens" and our parents were the "aliens."

Papa-san worried about the farm and our strawberry crop, which he planned to begin harvesting in late May. The timing was terrible.

"Couldn't they have waited until after we harvested our crop?" asked Papa-san. Then he sighed, resigned to the situation, and said, "Let's check with Mack and see if he would be willing to oversee the harvest."

Mack Garcia was a Filipino farm worker who had helped us for six years. He was one of thousands of Filipino men who came to the United States looking for work. Chinese and Japanese men had done the same thing years earlier before the U.S. government prohibited any more from coming.

The Chinese came to the United States in the mid-1800s to work on the railroads and do other lowly or dangerous jobs, such as mining. But when the railroads were completed and the Chinese began competing for jobs with the rest of the population, the U.S. Congress passed the Chinese Exclusion Act in 1882, which barred further Chinese immigration.

The Japanese later came to the United States to start a new life and work. However, the U.S. government's Exclusion Act of 1924 limited Japanese workers. Then in the early 1930s, the U.S. government allowed Filipino workers to immigrate.

Mack was in his mid-twenties when he started working on our farm. Papa-san welcomed him and was glad to have his help. We had a barn near the main house, and Papa-san converted it into a home for Mack. Papa-san paid Mack a fair wage, and Mama-san shared fresh produce from our garden with him.

"We should ask Mack to move into our home," suggested Mama-san. "I know he will do a good job making sure the berry picking is done properly."

And then she began to worry: "But he can't do that and all the administrative tasks that go with running the farm. Look how much it has taken all of us to run our place."

Yoneichi agreed. "Mack can't handle everything. Let me check with some of the other Japanese farmers and see what they plan to do."

The following evening at dinner, Yoneichi reported his findings. "There is a deputy sheriff on the island named G. H. Hopkins. He is willing to manage up to six farms. Ours will be one of them. Each farmer will work out his own arrangement with Hopkins regarding the terms of the relationship. In our situation, we should make Mack our boss in residence."

The deputy sheriff had been serving for years and had a good reputation. The Japanese people always respected authority and there was no reason to doubt Hopkins's integrity, but Yoneichi and Papa-san decided that a legal contract might be the best way to document the agreement—just in case. That would later turn out to be a wise decision.

The daily newspaper headlines continued to blast the Japanese for the death and destruction in the Far East. The war was not going well for the United States and the Allies. Radio reports repeatedly broadcast rumors of disloyalty and sabotage by Japanese-Americans on the West Coast. These rumors were false.

I grew more terrified that this inflammatory propaganda would cause people to riot against Japanese Americans. The world beyond Vashon Island seemed so dangerous, and now I would have to leave our harbor of safety. Part of me knew white people had always been my friends but now I began to question this. I couldn't accept they might hate me because I looked like the enemy.

All I wanted was for Japan and the United States to stop fighting and we could get back to living normally again. But that was not going to happen.

Even though I felt numb and in despair, I took heart in observing my parents. Their enduring Christian faith as well as previous experiences dealing with life's crises gave them strength. In turn, this gave me the example I would need to survive in the larger world beyond.

⊰◉⊱

Just a couple days before we had to leave, we got an urgent telephone call from our neighbor, Mr. Yamano. "Shizuko Ota died this morning," he said. "The funeral service must be held tomorrow afternoon before we leave in two days."

The news of Shizuko's death was unbelievable. She was only fourteen years old. The Otas were farmers, too. In addition to Shizuko, they had a son, Bill, sixteen years old.

Shizuko had **Downs Syndrome** and whenever I saw her at community gatherings I was put off by her unusual appearance and behavior. I would shy away from her, but I certainly took note of how kind Mama-san was and how gently she spoke to Shizuko.

Mrs. Ota treated Shizuko tenderly with the matter-of-fact efficiency of a busy farmer's wife. Usually, I saw Shizuko either beside her mother or aimlessly wandering in and out among groups of people. Shizuko was always dressed immaculately, like an exquisite doll. There seemed to be a quiet acceptance of this daughter who obviously was different from the rest of us young girls.

Mrs. Ota cried bitterly at the funeral. All of us were in such turmoil, so overwhelmed with dread of the future. In the end, all we could do was gather close together as the men used ropes to lower Shizuko's coffin into the ground. The memory of the family dropping clumps of earth into the grave would stay with me for a lifetime.

As we walked home after the funeral, the sky was clear and the warm air hinted of summer. After eating dinner and completing the evening chores, we went for a walk in pairs, Mama-san and me, and Yoneichi and Papa-san.

We walked the boundaries of our farm, admiring majestic Mount Rainier off to the southeast bathed in pink reflections from the sunset. Then we strolled down through the middle of our field, admiring the plump red strawberries almost ready to be picked. Each of us found a ripe one, bit into it, and savored the sweet fruit.

How we longed to be part of the hustle and bustle of the harvest. It was always so much work, but it was wonderful to look forward each year to seeing the same pickers. Together, we worked and laughed during the intense picking season. This year we would not be here.

Will we be back next year? I wondered. *And if not next year, when?*

Next, we stopped at the vegetable garden that Mama-san had planted. The lettuce was almost ready to eat and the peas were growing tall along the fence. We hoped Mack would enjoy the carrots and radishes. We lingered by the pink and white carnations, and I closed my eyes as I smelled the sweet blossoms.

Papa-san examined the fruit trees. The apple trees were beginning to bud, the nectarine tree looked as though it would have lots of fruit, and so would the fig vines.

We went to the barn to brush our horse, Dolly, who had worked so faithfully for us for many years. Next to the barn was the chicken coop. We threw some extra corn to the hens, who came clucking and scrambling to pick the choice grain.

Finally, we sat on the front porch in the deepening twilight, savoring our last evening of peace and home. We found comfort in each other's presence. Frisky, our faithful watchdog, and Kitty huddled beside us while we talked.

When we finally got up to go to sleep in our own beds one last night, I asked the great unknown, *How long will it be before we can come back? Will our farm still be here when and if we return?*

⊰◉⊱

Evacuation day came early. When I awoke after a fitful night's sleep, I lay still for a moment and took a deep breath, thinking, *This is the day.* It was May 16, 1942.

Mama-san was busy in the kitchen. The aroma of fresh coffee wafted upstairs. Reluctantly, I got out of my comfortable bed, smoothed the covers, and puffed up the pillow.

After I got dressed, I pulled up the window shade and looked outdoors. The sky was gray—a good reflection of how life appeared to me that morning. *Why do we have to go?* I asked no one. *Where are we going? When will we come back?*

My vision blurred. Slowly, I turned from the window and went downstairs.

"*Ohaiyo gozaimasu* (Good morning), Mama-san. This is the day, isn't it?

Mama-san nodded her head. *"Ohaiyo gozaimasu,* Mary-san. Yes, this is the day we have been planning for. Let's all sit down and have a good breakfast together before we leave."

All of us gathered for the last time around the kitchen table. We bowed our heads as Mama-san raised a brief prayer.

"Kami sama (God), thank you for the wonderful life we have shared here. We look to you as we begin another part of our lives. Guide us, sustain and strengthen us as we move ahead. Amen. Now, *itadaki masho.* (Let us eat.)"

Mama-san talked about how happy she had been in our home. As she talked, I wondered, *Why is she talking about happy times now?* But Yoneichi and Papa-san joined in, and soon we were all talking about the fun times we had shared on our farm.

We enjoyed our meal, then carefully tidied up the kitchen and our bedrooms. We laid out our suitcases side-by-side in the living room, checking our packed items one more time.

Finally, it was time to leave. Mama-san put on her hat, something she did only when going somewhere special. Instead of slacks and a shirt, she wore a pretty navy blue dress with a white crocheted collar along with **hosiery** and dress shoes. She carried a coat and purse. Papa-san wore his navy blue suit, white shirt, dress shoes, and a hat. Yoneichi dressed in a nice pair of slacks, a long sleeve dress shirt, Sunday shoes, and he carried a jacket. I wore a skirt and blouse, a sweater, and bobby sox with black oxfords.

We picked up our luggage and shut the door behind us.

One last time I patted Frisky and Kitty as I told them, "Help Mack and watch the house, okay?" Then silently, numbly, we moved away.

Frisky and Kitty sat on the back stoop, watching us. At the edge of our property we turned and took one final look through our tears at our beloved home.

CHAPTER SEVEN

FAMILY NUMBER 19788

The four of us walked in silence as we left our home.

Each of us carried two heavy suitcases. Anger and fear gripped my stomach. My thighs tightened as my toes grabbed at the earth—our earth—through the soles of my shoes. Above, barnyard swallows dipped and soared through the gray, still sky, twittering sporadically.

After awhile, I turned to Mama-san and asked, "Why do we have to leave? Why are they making us go?"

Mama-san turned her sad eyes toward me and quietly said, "Japan has attacked Pearl Harbor. There is fear that she will attack the West Coast. It is best that we leave."

Somehow, her answer didn't feel very satisfying. I had never been away from home, even to a friend's house, for more than one night. Now, I was leaving against my wishes, perhaps forever, and I didn't even know where we were going.

We lived on a berry farm on an isolated island. I was totally unprepared for any disruption to my life, much less one as big as this. We were among 120,000 Japanese Americans living in Western Washington, Oregon, California, and Arizona ordered to leave our homes.

I looked at Papa-san, who moved steadily forward, his eyes staring straight ahead, shoulders squared, lips pressed tightly together. A fixed look on his face hid the realization that he could not protect his family from this looming threat. Yoneichi mirrored our father, moving ahead with firm steps, his face sober, his jaws set firmly together.

Mama-san followed several paces behind, her sad eyes cast down. Dragging my feet, I walked beside Mama-san, feeling empty and confused. I was old enough to know that something was dreadfully wrong, but still frightened like a lost child. We said nothing.

I looked south to our neighbor's berry farm with its neat rows of currant bushes loaded with blossoms. Eleven years earlier when we first moved into our new home the McDonalds were the first to greet us. That evening they gathered several neighboring families to surprise us with a **shivaree**, a noisy celebration. We didn't know until then that the loud pounding of pots and pans and shouting was the typical way of welcoming newcomers in this rural community.

My family was overwhelmed by all of the good food and drink the neighbors brought us. This confirmed what my parents had told Yoneichi and me many times: "This is a wonderful country to live in." Although my parents were from a different country, it didn't matter to our Vashon neighbors. Their friendly welcome showed us they accepted people's differences.

Every spring after that shivaree, Mama-san took boxes of big, sweet, sun-ripened strawberries, the first and best of the season, over to the McDonalds and our other neighbors. That morning as we left our home, I wondered wistfully, *Will such a time come again?*

As we passed by the Peterson's home and their chicken ranch, I thought about how kind and understanding these neighbors had always been. Mr. Peterson was tall and lanky, but slightly stoop-shouldered from hunching over all the time tending to his chickens or their eggs. I used to buy eggs when our hens were not laying because the Petersons' chicken eggs were always fresh and good. Mrs. Peterson would invite me in for a cookie and a glass of milk whenever she saw me come for eggs.

One morning in the fifth grade, I missed the school bus and was running down the highway as fast as I could. Before I got a quarter of the way to school, Mr. Peterson came along in his pickup truck and stopped.

"Missed the bus, huh? Jump in."

Away we went, getting to school before the bus. These simple kindnesses loomed large as we walked away from our community, following government orders against our will.

When we were still about a quarter of a mile from Morita's, we were startled to see covered army trucks lined up along the street. Soldiers stood at attention with rifles and fixed bayonets. We all stopped. I couldn't believe what I was seeing.

Papa-san set his suitcases down without taking his eyes off the trucks. His eyes narrowed and his jaw tightened. "Army trucks." Under his breath he whispered, "I wonder what this means."

This was the first time I ever saw my father broken. Seeing him defeated terrified me.

Yoneichi's body stiffened and his face turned pale. He tightened his grip on his suitcases. He answered Papa-san in a clipped voice, "Yeah, looks bad." Yoneichi lowered his face, but his eyes remained fixed on the trucks, as if to ask, "Those guns, are they going to finish us off before we leave the island?"

Mama-san sucked in her breath and held it as all the color drained from her face. Seeing my family's reaction frightened me. I had to force myself to start walking again, asking myself repeatedly, *What have we done to deserve this?*

As we neared the designated area, it looked as if the soldiers thought some of us might resist or get out of hand. One soldier in particular watched my family as we approached. Holding his weapon in his right hand, his finger on the trigger, he pointed with his left to the place to deposit our luggage.

"Over there," he shouted, his upper lip curled into a snarl.

I couldn't let myself consider the possibility that the soldiers might take us away somewhere to shoot us. I wanted to cry but I didn't dare. I had to force myself to follow instructions.

We put our luggage together on the ground behind the trucks as directed. Another soldier with a much softer tone of voice gave us tags and our family number, 19788.

He looked at each of us and said, "Be sure to put that number on these tags and put them on each piece of luggage. You'll be identified as members of the same family, so be sure to put it on your coat or sweater, too, where we can see it."

MUSEUM OF HISTORY & INDUSTRY

Japanese Americans on Bainbridge Island wait for a ferry that will take them to Seattle, and on to an unknown destination. Soldiers oversee the evacuation.

The tag was to dangle clearly in view wherever we were. Now, I had become just a number—counted and labeled as the enemy.

◦◉◦

More families arrived. At the sight of the armed soldiers, they all looked frightened and whispered to each other. The children fell silent, huddling close to their parents. The adults were tight-lipped, their eyes darting from the soldiers to the guns to the line of army trucks nearby. I stood close to Mama-san and found comfort in our shared silence.

By 10:00 a.m. the Japanese families on Vashon Island—126 people in all—had gathered at specified assembly sites. The soldiers ordered us to climb aboard the trucks and insisted that we crowd close together. A sturdy box was in place for us to use as a step stool to climb aboard.

Yoneichi helped the older women as they took the gigantic step into the truck. Most were dressed in their finest Sunday clothes with silk stockings and nice shoes. One by one, we silently and grimly climbed aboard and sat on benches.

The soldiers piled our luggage around us before we started for the Vashon Heights dock. I took my place on the uncomfortable bench, avoiding eye contact with those across from me. I felt ashamed and dirty despite my tidy appearance.

The caravan of trucks snaked through the small town, past the Methodist Church that had been such a part of Yoneichi's and my life. We passed the Vashon Grade School and the gymnasium where I played with my friends. From inside the dark noisy truck that memory seemed a long time ago.

The ferry dock was familiar yet strange. Hundreds of people milled around with a sense of dread. I was stunned to see many of our non-Japanese neighbors and friends from church and school at the dock. They had gotten word of the evacuation and had come down that Saturday morning to say good-bye to us. As each of my classmates came forward for final words, I found it hard to say anything.

My classmate, Bob, came up and said, "Mary, I don't know what this is all about, but it all seems so unfair. I will really miss you. Do you know where you are going?"

"No, I have no idea."

Even Shirley, one of the most popular girls in our class, approached me and said, "Boy, this is terrible. Will you write to us so we can stay in touch?"

"I promise to do that," I responded, surprised that she would take the time to see me off. I didn't know she cared that much.

One of my closest Sunday school friends, Angie, said, "Take good care of yourself and your folks. We'll be praying for you."

"Thanks, Angie. I'll miss you."

But what I really wanted to say to Angie was, "I'll always remember that time you and your brother took me out on Puget Sound in your sailboat. It was so quiet and peaceful out there with the light warm breeze moving the boat gently through the smooth water. That was the only time I have ever been out on a sailboat and it was so much fun."

I couldn't bring myself to say it out loud for fear that I would cry uncontrollably.

A ferry finally arrived, but this was not the usual ferry we sailed all the time. It was smaller, old, and gray. Slowly it moved into place, then the workers tied it off and positioned a gangplank. I hugged my friends and said my tearful goodbyes. As I started down the gangplank, I had to blink several times to see where I was going. We descended into the unknown. It was now about 12:30 p.m.

The soldiers followed us aboard, then a worker raised the gangplank with a loud clang. As the ferry began to move out into the Puget Sound, everyone on the dock began to wave. Angie had one arm around her dad's waist as she waved her handkerchief with the other. She kept wiping her eyes with the handkerchief, calling out, "Goodbye, goodbye." The words floated across the waves as the ferry moved farther away.

My legs felt heavy, glued to the deck. I thought my lungs would burst from holding back my sobs. The voices from the dock became fainter and fainter until I could no longer hear them. The dock and the people grew smaller, but I couldn't stop looking until they disappeared.

⊱◉⊰

The ferry made another stop to pick up more families on the west side of Puget Sound at Kingston. It was late afternoon before we arrived at Pier 52 in Seattle. By then, I was exhausted from standing and staring for hours at the water.

Soldiers directed us toward a waiting train not far from the ferry landing. Onlookers gathered on the streets and the overpass nearby to watch us being escorted by armed soldiers.

We had to walk past the silent glaring crowd. I noticed a long string of cars parked along both sides of the street where we had to walk. My stomach knotted up when I saw a group of restless, angry-looking men with dirty coveralls standing along the sidewalk, each nervously fingering a shotgun.

One ruddy-faced, tall, heavyset man with deep vertical lines between his eyebrows acted like the leader. His steel gray eyes bulged as he lifted his gun with one hand and shook his clenched fist with the other.

"Get outta here, you goddamn Japs!" he shouted. "I oughta blast your heads off."

Dropping my eyes and head, I walked quickly past him. The other men didn't say anything, but they spat at us as we passed. Most of the crowd just stood and watched.

We walked to the train about 100 yards from the dock, not saying a word. I had never ridden on a train before. We boarded and looked for a place where we could sit together. Making my way down the aisle, I realized immediately these cars had not been used in a long time. There was a strong musty smell and the seats and floors were dirty. All the windows were shut and darkened to block the view outside. There would be no way of knowing where we were going.

Families tried to stay together and for the most part, this was possible. Eventually, everyone was aboard, including the soldiers. The train lurched forward into the night toward an unknown destination.

Looking around at everyone's grim and **stoic** faces, I felt afraid and frustrated that no one could say where we were going or why. There were so many people in our car, some standing in the aisles, we had to squeeze by one another to get to the restroom.

Once, when I tried to get back to my seat, I found that someone else had taken it. When I went looking for another place to sit, I found one on the top bunk of a sleeper car. There were many teenage girls sitting up there, none of whom I knew.

One of the tall, good-looking soldiers laughingly said to us as he walked down the aisle, "Hey, why don't some of you beautiful girls come three cars back to our car. There's plenty of room, and we've got some great grub, booze, and music. It'd be a heck of a lot more fun than being cramped up there."

One of the girls giggled and said, "Hmm, I wonder what that would be like."

Another answered, "Do you think we should go or not?"

"It sounds like it could be fun," the first girl replied. "It'd sure beat what we got here."

One of the girls asked, "Do you want to go for a little while, just to see what's back there?"

Something inside of me said, *No, that's not a good idea. I may be seventeen years old but I'm not ready for doing that sort of thing yet.*

Finally, two of the girls did get down and the last I saw of them they were worming their way toward the back. I have no idea what happened to them.

I began to worry if everyone in my family was going to the same place. Fear gripped my heart. *What would I do if we were separated from each other?* I thought. *What would become of my parents and what would become of me?*

We rode on the train for about three days, stopping occasionally. Soldiers distributed bagged meals, consisting of tasteless sandwiches, apples, and water.

Some of us thought we must have been going south because it kept getting hotter. At one point, I felt hot and cold simultaneously and slightly sick to my stomach. Then, I only saw blackness. A short time later, I awakened to see Mama-san and other people scurrying around me, wiping my face with a cool, damp cloth. Someone even got a window cracked open to let in some fresh air. That was the only time in my life I ever fainted.

≈ ⑥ ≈

We could not have known at that time that some families would have to live in hastily modified "assembly centers." People were forced to stay in livestock stalls and stables. Evacuation centers would include fairgrounds in Portland, Oregon, and Puyallup, Washington, and the racetracks, Santa Anita Park and Tanforan in California.

Years later, we learned that some of the people who were sent to these filthy places became very ill with vomiting and diarrhea because they had to live in livestock stalls soaked with animal urine and manure. In time, we would also learn about the severe prejudice and hatred other Japanese Americans faced, especially in California.

But that night, our train rumbled towards an unknown destination, carrying us to some place, for some unknown length of time—possibly to our death. Uncertainty was all we knew.

WORLD WAR II JAPANESE-AMERICAN INTERNMENT CAMPS & ASSEMBLY CENTERS

★ ASSEMBLY CENTERS & INTERNMENT CAMPS
WHERE MATSUDA WAS INTERNED

O OTHER ASSEMBLY CENTERS
■ OTHER INTERNMENT CAMPS
▲ ISOLATION CENTERS

This map shows the World War II internment camps and assembly centers in the United States where Japanese Americans were forced to go. Mary lived at Pinedale, Tule Lake, Heart Mountain, and Minidoka during the war.

CHAPTER EIGHT

THE FIRST INTERNMENT CAMP

Our train came to a stop shortly after noon on the third day of traveling.

Soldiers with rifles walked down the aisles and ordered us to get off. As I stepped off the train, I was startled to see that the landscape was entirely different from the lush green surroundings back home. Hills in the distance were shades of pale purple and brown. Wispy white clouds floated lazily in a stark blue sky. A faint sweet fragrance, unlike anything I had smelled before, wafted through the hot dry air.

There was no time for conversation. Soldiers barked orders to move ahead and climb aboard the covered army trucks. About twenty of us crowded into a truck. I was thirsty and had to go to the bathroom, but too fearful to ask.

As the truck moved away from the train, we could see miles of medium-sized trees in orchards. They were not like any trees we had ever seen before. Someone guessed they might be olive trees. We rode in silence for what seemed like hours, then the truck slowed down, turned, moved forward a short distance, and stopped.

A soldier shouted, "This is the end of the line."

Later, I would learn that we had arrived at Pinedale Assembly Center, a hastily built internment camp located eight miles north of Fresno, California.

Dorothea Lange, The National Archives

Japanese Americans carry their belongings to an assigned living space. Dust storms were common in many of the internment camps.

When I got off the truck I couldn't believe what I saw. Soldiers with machine guns stood in twenty-foot-high guard towers located along the perimeter of a huge camp. Steel wire fencing topped with three rows of barbed wire surrounded the whole camp.

Large searchlights next to the towers rotated continuously. Endless rows of black tar-papered barracks spread out along the flat terrain. Gray dirt or lava gravel completed the menacing scene. As we entered the camp, I stared at the barbed wire. *Why is the barbed wire facing inward?* I wondered. *Wasn't the government putting us here for our protection?*

Stunned by the sight, I stopped. Papa-san put his arm across my shoulder and gently guided me forward as he said softly, "Let's move ahead and find the place where we are to be."

Everywhere I looked there were hundreds of people with brown eyes, black hair, and yellow skin, just like mine. On Vashon Island, the majority of the people were white with a generous sprinkling of Japanese, Chinese and a few Filipino men. I had never lived in a place where everyone looked the same. People already living at the camp briefly glanced at us new arrivals with curiosity, disinterest or sympathy. Then they quickly dropped their eyes and moved on about their business.

Internees who had arrived much earlier helped us find the space we would try to make into a "home." All the barracks were identical, obviously constructed in a hurry. They had been framed up, the outsides sheeted with crude wooden siding, then covered with tarpaper. No additional siding was put over the tarpaper. The inside was plain wood sheeting. There was no plaster, paint, or insulation—just a blank, drab, tan room with four walls, a peaked roof, and an off-white concrete floor. A cow had obviously walked across the concrete floor before it had hardened, leaving her hoof prints.

Our living space was a bare 20-by-24-foot room in the middle of a 120-foot-long barrack. Our space had six army cots and a pile of blankets left in the middle of the room. Nothing else. No other furniture, no running water, no storage space, and nothing for cooking a meal. Only a single, bare light bulb screwed into a ceramic socket on the end of a long electrical cord hung from the ceiling. We would later learn there were five different sized living spaces in the building, all of them small and bare.

An older couple who had arrived just ahead of us was to share this same space with us. We were strangers to each other. Upon meeting, we looked at each other and silently nodded in acknowledgment. That nod between my parents and the older couple spoke volumes. The simple, nonverbal communication said how much we would see and not see, hear and not hear, smell and not smell as we lived four feet from each other. The nod meant, *We will honor your privacy.*

Partitions between the living spaces were only about seven feet high, leaving a four-foot triangular opening from the top of the partitions to the peak of the ceiling. This opening extended the full length of the barrack.

While we could not see our neighbors, we could hear every-thing that went on anywhere in the barrack, all the time. We could hear family quarrels, babies crying, laughter, hushed giggles, and at night snoring, coughing, and grinding teeth. All the sounds of humanity became background noise in the barracks.

We would soon begin to refer to these living spaces, about the size of storage rooms, as "apartments." All of the internees quickly adapted to finding nice ways to say difficult things when describing their imprisonment. Perhaps this was a way of cop-ing and maintaining some dignity. We were in a "camp," not a prison. We had "apartments," not prison cells.

On that first day, Papa-san and Yoneichi went off to find straw and **ticking** to make mattresses for each of our cots. Mama-san and I tried to figure out with the older couple how we should divide the space to accommodate our needs. We decided to hang army blankets to form walls so we could have some privacy.

Mama-san had always been a practical and optimistic person. Whatever her emotions were during our internment, she could adapt her frame of mind and feelings to the demands of the moment. In her characteristic manner, knowing that this was to be our "home," Mama-san matter-of-factly suggested we explore the camp to find out what was available to meet our basic needs. Silently I followed her outside to look around.

The central California sun was already very hot by late May. As we walked, a slight wind kicked up the fine dirt creating dust clouds. We found the mess hall, the men and women's bathrooms, showers, laundry room, and the recreation hall. Aside from these structures that had the same kind of construction as our barracks, there was nothing else in sight: no grass, trees, or flowers bloom-ing anywhere. Even the birds seemed to vacate the skies above our prison camp. People wandered about, all looking preoccupied, lost in disbelief of this barren environment.

Japanese-American evacuees were forced to live in horse stalls at an old racetrack converted into Tanforan Assembly Center. Many people got sick living in these filthy conditions.

◦◉◦

Pinedale was one of fifteen assembly centers set up for imprisoning Japanese Americans. Most of the assembly centers were in California. The government selected these sites because they had pre-existing facilities, including water, power, and sewage. This minimized the amount of construction required.

Fairgrounds and horse racetracks were often used. Poor construction practices were the norm, including the conversion of animal stalls into living spaces for families. The filthy and unhealthy living conditions caused illness and even death for some people.

We would later learn that Pinedale Assembly Center was actually better than some of the others. Pinedale was built on vacant land near an existing mill-workers housing area.

There were 4,823 people living in a five-block area, with each block containing 40 barracks. Each block had two mess halls equipped to feed 500 people in three shifts.

That first night at the assembly center we learned it was meal-time when a kitchen crewmember clanged a thick metal rod around the inside of a large triangle hung outside the mess hall door. Initially, my family didn't know what all that noise was for. We soon found out when we saw everyone walking toward the mess hall with their plates and utensils brought from home.

My family and I got in line outside the mess hall door. The line moved slowly. Once inside, I was amazed to see this huge hall packed with Japanese people of all ages. It seemed as though every-one was talking at once, a loud mixture of Japanese and English. Inching along, I finally got to the place where hot rice was plopped onto my plate followed by hot spicy chili and tossed salad. These were not things I would have chosen to eat in 100-degree heat.

The noise around us in the mess hall was deafening. I wanted to put my hands over my ears to shut out the pounding on my eardrums. Up to this point, the biggest crowd I had ever seen on Vashon was at our farm during holiday celebrations, and at school assemblies.

With all the noise and confusion of moving into this incredibly strange place and the hot mess hall, I had no appetite. I took a little of the salad, chewed it a long time, and finally swallowed, but it lodged in my throat and felt like it would go no further.

Mama-san said gently, "It's hard to eat, isn't it? But let's try to eat something—this may be all we will have today."

Our life on Vashon seemed so far away and long ago that first night at Pinedale. I had a great deal of trouble getting to sleep. The room felt like an oven, with not one cool breeze throughout the night. I could hear people tossing and turning on their cots, coughing persistently, and a tired baby wailing somewhere in our barrack. The continual sweep of the searchlight momentarily lit up the inside of our room with each rotation every few seconds. Each of us tossed and turned trying to find a comfortable spot on the straw mattress.

The next morning Mama-san and I went to the showers for the first time. They were located in a building that was divided in half: one end for men and the other for women. The shower building was unlike anything either of us had ever seen before. Multiple shower spigots hung from the ceiling. There was no privacy. All of us girls and women had to bathe in front of each other.

The first couple of times Mama-san and I took our showers, I felt very self-conscious. After turning the water on and waiting for it to heat up, I stood with my arms across my chest to hide my budding breasts. The exposure was difficult to adjust to. Later, we learned that some boys outside liked to peek at us through the knotholes in the boards while we showered. We quickly fixed that by standing watch for each other and holding our hands over these peepholes.

I thought about the conversation Mama-san and I once had about how she took baths in Japan.

"The bathtub in my childhood was located at the back of our home," explained Mama-san. "A deep wooden tub filled with water sat on a wooden platform. There was a small black door open at the bottom of the tub where coal burned in an iron container to heat the water in the tub. Beside it was a stool for us to sit on, a barrel of cool water, soap, and washcloth, and a dipper to pour water over our bodies after we had soaped and scrubbed thoroughly."

"Oh," I said, "you washed before you washed."

"Yes," Mama-san continued. "By doing it that way, all the dust and grime from the day is completely rinsed off and the hot water for soaking could be used by more than one person." She smiled at these pleasant memories. "It was the favorite time of the day for me."

How different and strange these public showers were from what I had known before. Bathing was a nightly ritual at our home on Vashon and it was done leisurely and with such pleasure, similar to how they bathed in Japan.

At the internment camp bathing wasn't "bathing" at all. It was a quick wash while someone stood guard against peeping toms. I quickly learned that every routine activity took extra thought and energy.

Using the latrine was one such activity. I figured out that I should get up early in the morning and hurry to the bathroom to brush my teeth. There was a long metal sink with water faucets located about every three feet for washing the hands and face. I went to the farthest end of the trough, away from the drain so I did not have to watch dozens of other people's frothy, yellowish saliva flow by me before going down the drain at the far end.

The bathrooms were divided similarly to the building for showers—one end for men, the other for women. The toilets were raised platforms with holes to sit over. There were partitions separating the stalls but no doors for privacy. It was so embarrassing for me to go to the toilet in such a public place that I would put it off until I really had to go.

The laundry room was a large common room. There were no washing machines, just scrub boards, deep sinks, soap, and lots of elbow grease. I often went with Mama-san to help with our weekly washing. She always greeted people pleasantly and knew the fine art of small talk without seeming insignificant. Throughout the laundry room pairs of women talked quietly to each other, gesturing, bowing, and nodding their heads. The laundry provided a place for them to gather to meet new people, share gossip, and complain. All conversation among my parents' generation, the *Isseis*, was in Japanese.

We had to eat all of our meals in the mess hall. There were no cooking facilities or running water in the barracks and no way for us to prepare any food in our room. How I missed our home cooked meals and family time around the dinner table! Mama-san was an excellent cook, but being a traditional mother, she never bragged about her delicious meals. I enjoyed working beside

People line up in front of a mess hall at Manzanar Internment Camp in order to get a meal. Families could not cook their own meals in their small living quarters.

her in our farm kitchen, whether it was shelling peas, cutting up vegetables, or making a special dish for dinner. In the internment camp, I spent a lot of time thinking about food memories.

⊰◉⊱

The days became hotter. Those of us from the cool Pacific Northwest were not used to the 100 to 115 degree heat. The desert sun sapped our energy, and we suffered especially when we had to line up outside the mess halls for our meals.

Fainting was a common occurrence. Some people showed concern when someone fainted, others did not unless it was a relative. The extremely hot climate and the strange, controlled environment of the camp added to everyone's agitation. People complained everywhere, every day.

Continuously, people asked questions that went unanswered by government authorities. "What about our fishing boats? The nursery? Our berry fields?"

My parents wondered about those very things, but they were more philosophical. Their responses were, "Yes, it is difficult, isn't it? I have those same concerns. All we can do now is hope that all this will end soon and we can all go home. *Shikata ga nai.* (It can't be helped.) *Gaman shimasho.* (Let us be patient.)"

I often wondered, *How can they be so calm and restrained?*

On reflection much later, I realized that was the way my parents had always looked at life—with thoughtful planning, patience, faith, and hope.

⋋◉⋌

One night around 4:00 in the morning I had to go to the bathroom. I put my coat on over my pajamas and slid my feet into my shoes before I headed for the bathroom.

Once outside, a huge bright light flashed on me. As I covered my eyes against the glaring light, I realized immediately that the searchlight at the nearby watchtower was focused on me. In the darkness, the searchlight had grabbed my privacy and exposed it to the camp guards. Blinded and stunned, I was powerless to stop the searchlight from bearing down on me. I ran back to the barracks. The light followed me and waited at the doorway as I hid, pressing my body against the inside wall of my family's living space.

Finally, the searchlight resumed its automatic circuit. Shaking in the darkness I realized, *I am seventeen and a prisoner of war in my own country.* I made myself wait until morning to go to the bathroom.

In the morning, I told my family what happened. Everyone looked grim. Yoneichi struck the bed with his fist. If he had been a swearing man, he would have cursed. Papa-san looked frustrated and powerless, unable to protect his daughter from the relentless searchlight. A shadow of pain flitted across Mama-san's face.

After a long silence, she spoke. "After this, whenever you have to go to the bathroom in the night, awaken me. I will go with you. I don't want you to go alone."

I agreed, and suggested that Mama-san call on me as well.

⋋◉⋌

At the internment camp, we got bits of news that the war in the Pacific and Southeast Asia was going badly for the Allies. I didn't want to think about the possibility that the camp soldiers might kill us all because we looked like the people they were fighting in the war.

I could not let myself think that this is what some people in the U.S. government might want to do. I lived in constant fear. It was a surprise whenever someone laughed or more so, when I laughed. Jokes or funny stories were not a part of daily conversation.

Back home Yoneichi had always been the clown in our family. Periodically, he would make us all laugh by imitating different characters he had heard on the radio or seen in the movies. He sounded and looked like Donald Duck when he quacked and waddled around the house. He would flex his biceps like Popeye as he sang, "I'm Popeye the Sailor Man." Or he would imitate Woody Woodpecker's famous laugh: "hahaHaHAha!"

There was no one laughing at the Pinedale internment camp. The barbed-wire fence, soldiers in guard towers, and continuously rotating searchlights were somber reminders of our imprisonment. I realized I was in prison because of what I looked like, and because I shared a certain lifestyle and culture with a people an ocean away. The most sobering realization was that the U.S. Army and government could do this to American citizens. An executive order could take us away in shame and we had no recourse. Our government held the ultimate power.

I began to question, *If this could happen to us, couldn't it happen to anyone?*

Daily, I struggled to understand, *Why are we treated like criminals and outlaws?* My soul wept silently because it was safe only if I was silent, obedient, and cloaked in numbness.

‹CHAPTER NINE›

MOVED AGAIN

"**P**ack up your things, you're leaving tomorrow for a permanent camp," the soldiers told everyone.

Startled, I said to Papa-san, "A permanent camp? Was this only
a temporary place?"

We had been at Pinedale only a month and a half. "Where will
we have to go this time?" I continued. "And how permanent is
'permanent'?"

Papa-san looked down and was silent. Finally, he raised his
tired eyes and said, "I don't know, Mary-san. We'll just have to
wait and see what happens."

By now, I was starting to get exasperated that Papa-san didn't
have the answers either. In the past, he had always known what
to expect, and it was frightening to see him as helpless as I was.
I hoped desperately that wherever we were going, we could be
together.

The train ride out of Pinedale, though stressful, was at least a
break from the boring routine we had endured at the Pinedale
camp. The old train cars were musty, dirty and creaky, just like
the last train. As before, the windows were darkened and we
could not look at the passing landscape. How I wished we could
have seen signs of normal life.

Rocking back and forth on the old seats, we were all lost in our thoughts. We hardly spoke. My periodic trips to the restroom took me past several families from Vashon quietly huddled together. The Aoyama family sat with bowed heads. Mrs. Aoyama, one of Mama-san's closest friends from home, nodded to me each time I passed.

When I passed a friend from Vashon, Ardith Kumamoto, I raised my hand slightly and tried to smile. She was sitting with her parents and her three sisters. Ardith was a petite, pretty girl with big dark eyes and long eyelashes. We had become good friends because we used to perform Japanese dances together back home.

From the time Ardith was in the fifth grade and I was in the fourth grade, we went weekly to Mrs. Nakamura's Japanese dance class. We would practice for performances in Japanese community events. It was the only time I could dress up and wear a touch of lipstick.

One time, Ardith's father took us for a ride in their black, shiny touring car with the top folded down. In the 1930s, cars were still a novelty on the island, and getting a ride was a real treat. Ardith and I giggled as we sat together in the back seat anticipating our ride. When the car leapt forward we sat back to enjoy the wind on our faces. What an incredible sense of freedom! Ardith and I raised our arms and cheered wildly.

Seeing my neighbors' faces on the train took me to thoughts of Vashon and home. How I missed the island lush with evergreens, surrounded by the blue waters of Puget Sound. How I longed for a drink of pure, cool water from our well. How innocent I had been in that peaceful environment.

~◎~

The tension on the train heightened abruptly when the locomotive blew its whistle and slowed to a stop. We had been riding for about a day and a half.

A soldier suddenly appeared at the end of the car. "Okay, everybody off," he barked.

People slowly got out of their seats, grabbed their luggage, and began filing out one by one. I followed those ahead of me to the doorway, then stopped when I saw where we were headed. I was overwhelmed. This camp looked ten times bigger than the last one and I felt one hundred times smaller.

My stomach churned and my chest tightened as I looked at a blur of black barracks separated by huge bare spaces. Later, I found out that the purpose of the wide, bare ground was to create firebreaks between the flimsy wooden barracks.

WING LUKE MUSEUM

Internment camp barracks were all similar. This is a photo of Minidoka Internment Camp.

The firebreaks divided the camp into seven wards. Most of the wards were made up of nine blocks; each block had fourteen barracks. There were 64 blocks altogether. With approximately 260 men, women and children per block, we had a population of more than 18,000 people at this new internment camp. I had no idea there were so many Japanese people living in America!

We had arrived at Tule Lake Relocation Center, located twenty-six miles south of Klamath Falls, Oregon. Despite its name, I never saw a lake anywhere near the internment camp.

Like Pinedale Assembly Center, this camp was encircled with a high chain-linked fence topped by three rows of barbed wire, all slanted *inward*. Soldiers with machine guns watched us from tall guard towers. These lookouts were equipped with large mounted searchlights that continuously swept across the camp throughout the night.

A *Nisei* man drove us to our "space," which was 7404 C (block 74, barrack 4, apartment C) in the northwestern corner of the camp. The barracks here were similar to those at the Pinedale Assembly Center: 120 feet long, divided into varying sized "apartments," which were nothing more than rectangular rooms with openings above the seven foot walls. These open spaces extended the full length of the barrack. Any sound made in any one of the living cubicles could be heard throughout the barrack.

When we got to our 20-foot by 20-foot space, I remarked to my family, "Look, the room is smaller but we don't have to share it with anyone else. That's good."

Our parents silently nodded. Looking at the pot-bellied stove, Yoneichi commented, "Must get cold here." The flimsy barrack walls would scarcely protect us from the subfreezing temperatures. That winter the doorknob would get so cold our fingers would stick to it.

Japanese Americans who came first—mostly from Sacramento, California—had already occupied the central part of the camp. Those of us from Washington and Oregon were sent either to the northwestern section of the camp or the southeastern part. Later, this would become significant. I would quickly realize that I felt more comfortable spending time in our own area with people from the Northwest and especially from Vashon.

⋰◉⋱

My initial shock at seeing the camp for the first time gave way to depression as reality set in. We were going to be here for awhile, perhaps forever for all I knew.

There was a notice posted in our "apartment" that gave the name of the block manager of our barracks, what his duties would be, and his office location. The note asked us to come to his office to identify ourselves and to sign up for various jobs that needed to be filled.

After we looked around the camp and went to the block manager's office, we came home to compare notes. The camp layout was similar to Pinedale.

Yoneichi announced proudly, "Mr. Mayeda from Vashon is going to be the chief cook in our mess hall. I asked him if I could be his assistant and learn how to cook. He agreed, so now I've got a job. I'll get paid $16 a month."

Professional people like doctors, lawyers, dentists, and chief cooks were paid at the highest rate of $19 a month. Semi-skilled workers received $16 and unskilled laborers $12 per month.

Papa-san and Mama-san signed up as janitors for the school that was to be set up. They would each be paid $12 a month. I signed up as a waitress at $12 a month to serve breakfasts and dinners during the school year, and all meals during the summer. Since I had only worked on the farm to help my family and did not receive an allowance, $12 a month didn't sound too bad to me, especially given what everyone else got paid.

While Papa-san waited to begin work as a janitor, he signed up with the road crew and was active every day. Yoneichi was busy learning to cook meals. Mama-san and I helped clean up in the mess hall after each meal. Each of us found ways to fill our time.

Because of the highly structured way of life in camp there was nothing specific for most people to do. Many drifted about aimlessly. If they were back at their homes they would have been working from dawn to dusk at their farms, greenhouses, hotels, restaurants, or whatever they did to make a living. In camp, there were many tasks such as garbage collection, fire station watches, and block manager work, but all of these were quickly assigned.

Later, the need for adult education classes, arts and crafts, and other creative outlets would become obvious. For now, the overwhelming social problem was simply that there was nothing to do.

The *Isseis* in particular had a powerful work ethic that made them successful in their careers back home. Many had not taken a proper vacation in years or even in decades. For some, the initial weeks at the internment camp with the idle hours were a welcome relief. Before long, they discovered that time had to be filled with activities they considered unimportant, such as sitting around and talking, doing needlework for hours, going to the laundry room or mess hall, or just standing around complaining. Our stress came from not having enough to do.

Papa-san was an adaptable man. He met others in the block and before long he was part of an older men's group who played *Go*, a Japanese board game. Two players alternately placed flat, round, black or white stones on the board. The strategy was to trap the

This is a typical mess hall in the internment camps. Families brought their own plates, cups and eating utensils with them.

other player within a given area by surrounding the opponent's stones with one's own. Whenever a game was going on, observers stood close to the players and watched in rapt silence.

To fill my time after my daily waitress job, I got out the little radio I had brought from home and listened to a program called "Voice of Prophecy." It was a conservative fundamentalist Christian program that I thought could help me find some answers to my desperate questions: *Where does it say that Jesus is the Savior? What do I have to do to be saved from this terrible place?*

I needed comfort, direction, and hope, but all I heard on "Voice of Prophecy" were words. The words gave me no hope that this would all end soon. Still, I kept listening carefully, redlining passages in my Bible that were particularly meaningful. *There must be some answers somewhere,* I told myself.

I knew my parents were deeply spiritual people. I wished I was, too. I searched the Bible but I couldn't find the key to help me. *I will just have to keep looking,* I decided. My parents didn't object to my listening to the sermons but I think Mama-san saw my preoccupation with the Bible and my isolation from others as unhealthy.

On more than one occasion she urged me, "Mary-san, let's go outside into the sunshine and go for a walk. I think it will be better for us to get out and see what is out there. We might find something interesting and meet people."

I longed for Vashon's warm spring days when the fog disappeared in the bright sunshine. I especially missed our green lawn where I stretched out after a day's work and watched lazy white clouds float across the sky. My classmates at school and my friends at the church seemed a world away.

❧❧❧

During our imprisonment in the Japanese-American internment camps, we did not hear about the concentration camps in Europe and the Nazis murdering millions of Jews and other groups of people. I knew the United States and its allies were fighting Nazi Germany, but I had no idea the Nazis used their terrible belief of "racial superiority" as a reason to kill groups of people they decided were "inferior." This included Gypsies, Slavic people from Poland, Russian prisoners-of-war, people with mental and physical disabilities, homosexuals, Jehovah's Witnesses, Communists, and Socialists. This mass murdering of human beings would be called "The Holocaust."

The Japanese Americans in internment camps had it far better than the Jews in Nazi Germany's concentration camps where millions died. However, if I had known of their plight at the time, fear for my own life may have pushed me over the edge. Even without knowing the details of The Holocaust, I was constantly afraid in the internment camps of being shot or killed.

CHAPTER TEN

LAST DANCE IN
THE SEARCHLIGHT

Dust storms plagued the Tule Lake internment camp.

These unpredictable dust storms came and went as if the desert kept throwing furious tantrums. Suddenly, we would all have to run for shelter, covering our faces with handkerchiefs or clothing to block the dust from our faces. Then, just as suddenly, the dust storm would stop. Even the slightest breeze could pick up the dirt and swirl it around the barracks, chasing us as we scrambled for cover.

After we had been at Tule Lake for a few weeks, I learned that my dance instructor, Mrs. Nakamura, had been asked to present a program at an upcoming outdoor event. She was well known in Seattle as an instructor and player of the *shamisen,* a Japanese stringed instrument.

These programs at the internment camp were the first attempts to relieve people's boredom by using the talents of the community. My friend from Vashon, Ardith, and I were selected to perform. Mama-san was very pleased and so was I. It was a great honor, but I wasn't sure about dancing in front of a large and unfamiliar audience.

Ardith and I practiced together every day. We followed Mrs. Nakamura's instructions precisely as she strummed on the *shamisen.* Listening and dancing to the rhythm of the music, I escaped from the dreariness and fear of the camp. It reminded me of the many times Ardith and I practiced together in our teacher's spacious living room on Vashon.

Whenever I danced to the traditional Japanese music I had a vision of a person quietly walking beside a gentle stream trickling over rocks. The water followed the bends in the river, finally flowing into a calm pool. The music and the movements took me to a peaceful place where my two cultures—Japanese and American—unified for a brief time. When I danced I felt whole—Japanese by heritage and American by birth.

Ardith and I moved slowly and gracefully making each step with the bend of the knees. Each head, arm, and hand movement, each turn of the body, flowed together into the next position. We practiced until Mrs. Nakamura felt confident in our movements. I was delighted to have her approval.

The evening of our performance finally arrived. Several ladies helped us put on our beautiful kimonos. Mrs. Nakamura had borrowed the kimonos from some families who had brought them to camp. Ardith's had red, purple, and gold leaves on a beige background with a red *obi*, a sash, interwoven with silver threads. Mine was a dark blue kimono with soft, simple patterns in gray. My *obi* was also red with silver threads.

Getting dressed in kimonos is a lengthy, complicated process. I was prepared to stand for quite awhile as the ladies tugged and pulled the sashes around me.

First came the short-sleeved undershirt tied at the waist, followed by the under robe, which is long and visible only at the neck like the collar of a shirt. Next we put on the kimono, which is heavy and long. It must be folded up and tied with a cord to hold it in place.

This was followed by a wide long *obi*, which the women wound tightly around my waist several times making it impossible to take a deep breath or take long bold steps. Then they tied the *obi* into a special knot on my back and held it in place with various cords and clasps. With white *tabi* (Japanese socks), and *geta* (wooden clogs) on our feet, and red lipstick, we were ready.

Mama-san gave me her last minute advice, "This is an opportunity to represent the Vashon Japanese community, so do your very best."

We arrived at the outdoor platform where a crowd had gathered to watch our performance. It was almost unbearably hot in my heavy kimono. The late afternoon air was stifling as the sun set. Mrs. Nakamura, dressed in her muted colored kimono, stepped onto the stage and seated herself on a chair. Holding her *shamisen* on her lap, she smiled and nodded at us confidently.

As I approached the platform in my beautiful kimono, my stomach fluttered, but I was full of energy. Ardith and I took our positions in the center of the stage and waited to begin our dance. In that moment, I knew we brought hope to the audience, representing the beauty and value of our culture.

Suddenly, the revolving searchlight from a nearby guard tower flashed across my face. I dropped my eyes and froze momentarily, blinded. My legs felt heavy, my arms like stone. I struggled to regain my composure.

As I waited for the cue to begin, I told myself, *Listen for the first stroke on the shamisen. Concentrate on each step. Remember what Mama-san said.*

I glanced out over the crowd in the direction towards Mama-san. She looked at me, smiled, and nodded her head.

On the third strum of the music I slowly turned my head to the right and raised my right hand higher than my left in front of my body. My hands opened like the wings of a crane. Bending my knees slightly, I slowly slid my right foot slightly ahead of my left.

Forget everything else and move with the twang of the music, I told myself. *You know the steps by heart.*

As if suspended in time and space, I numbly and automatically made each movement. Slowly, slowly, and step by step we moved.

Gradually, the movements of my body and the rhythm and tone of the *shamisen* took over until I realized that Ardith and I were dancing well together. Relief, self-confidence, and even some self-importance finally crept back in as I gained a sense of the appreciative audience. I had finally found my own place in this barren camp.

We had only been dancing a couple of minutes when suddenly, a blast of hot wind whipped up the fine dust, swirling it everywhere. Dust swooshed across the open spaces and between the barracks, enveloping us on the exposed, elevated platform. It felt like a thousand bees were stinging our hands and faces. We could taste the dirt and grit, barely able to breathe.

Mrs. Nakamura stopped playing. We covered our noses and mouths, and scrambled off the platform in our beautiful kimonos. Everyone scattered like leaves before a giant blower.

Ardith and I took cover behind the closest barrack. By then, Ardith's hair and kimono were coated with fine dust. It clung to the bangs on her forehead, to her eyelids and eyelashes, and stuck to her lipstick. Tears ran down her dusty cheeks. When Ardith brushed the tears aside, the dust left a smudge across her cheek. I must have looked like a dust ball myself. Then the storm died down as abruptly as it had started. We each ran back to our barracks.

When I got home, dust had penetrated through the cracks in the loose-fitting window, under the door, and up through the floorboards. Like thick smoke that streamed out of a smoldering fire, dust seeped through everything in its path, finding and filling every nook and cranny.

It seemed as though God Himself was saying, "No."

I wasn't accepted in the white community, but when I tried to be Japanese, I felt crushed. I threw myself on my cot and sobbed. Mama-san sat down beside me, lifted me into her arms and silently rocked me back and forth, back and forth, until my crying subsided.

Later, we cleaned our apartment, then stuffed paper into every crack we could find. But that didn't help. There was always dust everywhere—the dark cloud that invaded every aspect of our life at the camp.

⤞◉⤝

This was the last time Ardith and I danced together. Before the year was over, we would be separated forever. My family would be sent to the Heart Mountain Relocation Center in Wyoming and Ardith's family would go to the Topaz Relocation Center in Utah.

Ardith's ultimate goal was to travel to the East Coast to be with Hanako, her older sister. Our letters flew back and forth for months. Then they stopped.

Months after our dance in the dust storm a letter came from Hanako telling me that Ardith had died from an unknown disease. When I read that, I rushed outdoors, stumbling and looking at the barbed-wire fence. I raised my clenched fists into the air and shouted "Ardith" in anguish.

A strong wind swooped down, picking up the fine dirt and sent it surging through the air, blinding me. I took cover behind the closest barrack and crumpled to the ground, sobbing.

Eyes closed, I pictured Ardith's large beautiful eyes, her black shiny hair against her clear, creamy skin. *How beautiful and graceful she looked as she danced with me on the stage,* I thought. *I will never see her again.*

Our dance in the searchlight was Ardith's last. In that moment, I decided it would be my last dance, too.

CHAPTER ELEVEN

DIGNITY IN THE MIDST OF HARDSHIP

Days of the week no longer mattered.

The mess hall gong broke up the slow hours of the day, calling us to breakfast, then lunch, and dinner. I was tired all the time, so I slept a lot. I lay on my cot for long periods of time or wandered aimlessly outdoors. I had little energy or interest in making friends or participating in any activity. My days simply came and went.

It was now August, three months since our evacuation from Vashon. One evening after dinner when I was feeling especially low and confused, I told Mama-san I wanted to talk to her in private.

We walked briskly back to the empty apartment. Papa-san lingered at the mess hall visiting with friends from Vashon, and Yoneichi was busy cleaning up in the mess hall kitchen.

Mama-san sat down on her cot and I plopped down opposite her on mine. Without a moment's hesitation I plunged into my dilemma.

"I thought I was being a good citizen and helping in the war efforts by going along with the evacuation process."

"Yes," Mama-san replied. "You were."

"But," I insisted, "instead of feeling good for having done my part and being rewarded, I feel double-crossed. I thought every American citizen was supposed to have life, liberty, and the pursuit of happiness. That's what we were told in school back home, but that isn't what we have here."

Mama-san listened thoughtfully as she usually did, then responded gently, "Mary-san, we are in the middle of something that is much bigger than any of us. America is at war in many parts of the world. Things are difficult for lots of people everywhere."

WING LUKE MUSEUM

Guard towers were typical in all the internment camps. Soldiers with guns and searchlights kept people in the camps. This one was at Tule Lake.

"I don't care! I don't like it here!" I choked up as I tried to make my point. "There's nothing to do here! I'm tired of the dust storms, these awful meals, and no privacy! I don't like anything about this place! I thought we would be here for a short time, but now it's lasting forever!"

"I understand, but we are not the only ones suffering," Mama-san replied, still calm. "There is much misunderstanding and misery in all of the camps, I'm sure. This is the time for us to *gaman shimasho* (be patient)."

Then she added, "*Shikata ga nai*. (It can't be helped.) We must do our very best to do what seems right every day."

"But I don't want to wait," I snapped back. "I'm tired of waiting. I want to go home now. I want to get away from this awful place."

Hot tears stung my eyes.

Mama-san dropped her eyes for a moment, then looked up. She took a deep breath and said, "Some day the war will end and we will be able to go home. Then we will understand more. I know this is very hard for you, but it will all work out all right eventually. Have faith."

I wanted to believe she was right, but I couldn't get past the feelings of dread and anger whenever I looked at the soldiers in full combat uniform holding their guns. Everywhere we went, the soldiers watched us from their towers.

Mostly, what I couldn't get over—and couldn't talk about—was my deep fear that someday when I least expected it, the soldiers would come and kill us all.

≺◉≻

On September 14, 1942, Tri State High School and an elementary school were opened at Tule Lake internment camp. I was now a senior and I looked forward to finishing high school. I signed up for Typing I, English IV, Latin II, Problems of Democracy, Physical Education, Chemistry, and Senior Problems.

When I went to my English IV class, I was startled to see a white male teacher in the room. I looked around for books, pencils, paper, and other supplies. I didn't see anything. The only person with a book was the teacher. Embarrassed, I sat on one of the benches in the second row and waited awkwardly until some other students came and sat down, too

Later, I found out there were other white teachers who came from "the outside" to teach some of the classes. Some teachers were *Niseis* who had their teaching credentials before they came to camp. But for both of these groups of teachers, it was difficult. All classes were held in barracks, and students sat on hard benches or on the floor. At first, there were no supplies for teachers, no typewriters for typing classes, no lab equipment for chemistry, and no blackboards.

In my typing class the teacher had drawn the keyboard on a large piece of paper and placed it at the front of the class. We learned by "typing" on our laps in what must have been the quietest typing class in history. The chemistry class ran without test tubes, chemicals or other essential parts of a laboratory. We had to imagine

The first high school at Tule Lake. A name had not yet been chosen.

mixing certain chemicals to produce certain outcomes. It was a challenging situation for everyone.

One of the hardest parts of going to school took place first thing every morning when I stood outdoors with other students in front of an American flag.

We had to place our hands over our hearts and recite, "I pledge **allegiance** to the flag of the United States of America…one nation, indivisible…" I stumbled over the words "with liberty and justice for all."

How strange it felt to be saying the Pledge of Allegiance after a forced evacuation to a prison camp.

After classes were out on the first day of school, I went straight home to talk with Mama-san. She was wearing a freshly ironed blue and white striped dress and sitting on her cot reading the newspaper.

"Do you know what we had to do this morning?" I asked heatedly as I dropped down on the cot across from her. I didn't think about how loud my voice must have sounded throughout the whole barrack.

"No, I have no idea." Mama-san looked up at me with interest in her eyes.

"We had to pledge allegiance to the American flag. I could see the barbed-wire fence in the background. I don't think we should have to do that here, do you?" I asked bitterly.

Of course, there had been hundreds of times that I enthusiastically repeated the pledge back home, but we all did it without giving a thought to what it represented.

Mama-san glanced down and was thoughtful for a minute. Finally, she lifted her eyes and said, "I can see your point. It's difficult to pledge your allegiance to a country that treats us this way, isn't it? What do you think you should do about it?"

I gathered all my strength and did something I never would have considered doing before. We didn't use swear words in our family but I steeled myself and blurted out, "Well, I'd really like to tell them they're full of bullshit and not say the Pledge of Allegiance!"

Right away, I knew I had gone too far. Mama-san's body stiffened, her lips parted in surprise. It was the first time I had ever approached her in what she might think was a tantrum. Swearing meant losing one's temper, but I wanted her to know how mad I felt.

I could see her searching for just the right words. Soon her face relaxed and her eyes softened as she said, "Yes, you could do that. And what would that do?"

"It would make me feel a whole lot better."

"Yes, I'm sure it would." She cocked her head to one side, and glanced past me for a moment. "But would it change anything?"

Her question disoriented me. I hunched my shoulders and looked at the floor to think about that a minute before I finally looked up. It was my turn to choose the right words.

"I don't know if anyone else feels the same way I do. And even if they did, I'm not sure they'd do anything about it right now anyway." In a much quieter tone I added, "I don't know, I suppose not."

"You're probably right. I don't think it would change a thing either," Mama-san agreed. "You know there are times to be patient and persevere. This is one of those times."

Pondering this for awhile with all the feelings whirling around inside of me, I finally said, "That's going to be awfully hard to do."

I didn't want to make a big fuss over this with my mother. A part of me knew she was right, but in my heart I didn't want to be patient and persevere. I kept thinking, *This isn't right! They shouldn't make us do it!*

In her youth, Mama-san had studied ancient Japanese history. Her familiarity with Japan's history gave her the ability to look beyond this war camp and to see the bigger picture. While everyone else was caught in the suffering of the moment, she knew that with time, these events would make a different kind of sense.

For now, I had to trust what Mama-san said, even though I couldn't see an end to our plight.

⊰◉⊱

Every day we were in our drab little room with our four army cots and a potbellied stove. Our suitcases served as bedside stands. Papa-san had made a simple table with scrap lumber he found. We pounded some nails into the wall by the door to hang our coats. To make it a little more cheerful, Mama-san had purchased some fabric from the store at the prison camp. She hand sewed curtains with bright red and yellow flowers and green leaves on a white background. She also made a curtain for the front of a wood crate that we used as a cupboard.

But every evening when I looked at the one light bulb screwed into a ceramic socket on the end of the long cord hanging from the ceiling, I felt unhappy and confused. For long stretches I just sat on my bed and stared at the bare bulb.

Looking at the light reminded me of home. My memories of home became my refuge from the ugliness of the camp. I was not the only one who thought often about Vashon. One night as I was lying on my hard cot, Yoneichi whispered, "Still awake?"

"Yeah," I said.

"Whatcha thinking about?" he asked, as he flopped down on his cot.

"Home."

"Yeah, I figured," he said. "I think about it a lot, too. We'd be finishing up trimming and tying up the loganberry canes right about now, if we were back on the farm."

Talking with Yoneichi, I realized I even missed the fights. There were times when Yoneichi and I would get into an argument about some silly little thing.

Home. I couldn't stop thinking about it. I loved to look to the east in the morning and watch the changing hues of pink on Mount Rainier. In the evenings, the setting sun painted the western sky with a scarlet brush that gradually turned reddish-blue, then blue, and drifted into a deep purple before it faded away. As thousands of stars emerged, a peace descended upon the land. Before I went to sleep, I would get into a tub of warm water and soak for as long as I wished. Home was where I felt safe.

That whole world had dissolved like an illusion. Now, the only reason to get up in the morning was to go to classes and do the mess hall chores I had signed up for. I tried to study hard and stay up with my classes, but time hung over me, empty and meaningless; there seemed no point in living.

It wouldn't be until years later that I would realize how deeply the events of this time in my life would affect me forever. At the time, I went through the motions of the routine without really knowing who I was.

As was common for the oldest son in the Japanese culture, Yoneichi had been encouraged to be assertive and initiate contact with others. As the daughter, I was more retiring and supportive.

School children march through camp with American flags to show their
patriotism. Minidoka, 1943.

In our new environment, Yoneichi continued to reach out. He
would go off and find others with whom to play ping pong, vol-
leyball, baseball or just talk. It was easy for him to make friends
and move among the young and old. I envied him.

For me, it seemed difficult to get hold of anything meaningful.
Whenever I wasn't in school, I spent most of my time in our barrack
sleeping or daydreaming. I withdrew from the world. It was a world
I needed to escape. Mama-san became concerned.

One night, I awakened and overheard my parents talking.
Mama-san said softly to Papa-san, "I'm worried about Mary-san.
She seems so miserable and quiet." Papa-san agreed.

"This experience seems to be overwhelming her," Mama-san
added.

I wondered, *Do they know I am awake listening to their conversation?*
Are they having this talk for my benefit or for themselves? I held my
breath as I listened, afraid they might judge me or be disappointed.

Papa-san let out a long breath. "I wish we could ease it for her.
This is Mary-san's first taste of *haiseki* (prejudice). It's a big dose

to swallow all at once." He was silent for a moment, then added thoughtfully, "If she can just get through this, an experience like this could make her into a stronger person."

Suddenly, it struck me that he had faced prejudice far worse than I had ever experienced. I was facing a test. I asked myself, *Would I do something to shame my family and myself? Would I fail them?*

"I hope she can learn from this. I'd like to see her develop strength so that she can face whatever will come in her life," Mama-san replied.

Papa-san sighed again. "You and I know we're not alone in this. We know that God is even here, but life brings different kinds of pain to everyone, and each of us has to find our own way to cope."

"That's true, but it's so sad to watch," admitted Mama-san. "Mary-san had no choice in the matter. I know it does no good to look at it that way, but still, it makes my heart ache." Her voice broke.

I, too, struggled with my own emotions of anger and grief. Hearing how they felt, how could I blame them? I just felt sorry for myself. And yet, scared.

"Yes, I know," Papa-san replied gently, "but that's the way it is. We have to go on from here. Mary-san has to get used to being with our people—right here, right now. It would be different if she had grown up in California where *haiseki* (prejudice) by the white people is more obvious. The Japanese there got used to it and figured out how to band together for moral support to look out for their interests. We thought we were so lucky living on Vashon where our kids were protected. If we had lived in California, this would not be such a shock to her."

As I listened to their conversation in Japanese, I realized again how formally they were speaking to one another. Not all Japanese families spoke this way, but it was my parents' way of caring for their family as well as others.

I was amazed at how my parents could be so optimistic and strong at a time when it was so easy to complain and criticize the government. At the time, I thought they were just being patient, but looking back I see that their dignity and inner strength were bone-deep in their character. Dignity was what defined who they were. Each of them had made a decision to face hardship when they left their homeland, but it pained them to see me facing hardships I had never chosen.

When my parents were done talking, they said, "*Oyasumi nasai*" (good-night) and settled in to sleep.

In the quiet, the tension in my chest subsided. My parents were keeping the world solid for me. I didn't feel so alone anymore.

I told myself, *If they can handle it, I can handle it.*

Tears flowed freely down my cheeks and onto my pillow. The knot in my stomach released. *How lucky I am to have them for my parents.*

In a world so mixed up, my parents were very clear about who they were. Their faith that it would all work out was profound. Their love was stronger than my fear.

Finally, I drifted off into my first restful sleep since we left home. Years later as I reflected on this conversation between my parents, I realized what a gift they had given me. We were all in this together. Bathed in their unconditional love and respect, my fear and depression decreased. They had given me a future, a model for my life.

CHAPTER TWELVE

COLLECTING SEASHELLS
AT TULE LAKE

Still in bed after missing breakfast, I was stuck in my unhappiness, daydreaming about home.

Mama-san walked in and said, "Mary-san, I was talking to one of the ladies in the restroom. She told me there are lots of shells about two blocks from here. There are shells everywhere. Let's go and see how many we can find, *neh?*—all right?"

I looked up at her and was touched by the concerned look on her face. I didn't want to get out of bed, but I wanted to do something to reassure Mama-san that I'd be okay. Thinking about my parents' conversation I had overheard two nights before, I agreed.

We started a daily, early morning ritual of shell collecting before the heat of the day. I was surprised to see many other women and girls searching, too. Perhaps we were all looking for beauty or something that spoke of other times and survival.

About 13,000 years ago Tule Lake was a freshwater lake, but now it was bone-dry sediment and silt with thousands of tiny seashells. As we looked for shells, it was easy to move the dirt from side to side. A handful of lake sediment might contain as many as thirty shells. Most of them were spiral-shaped, white, and tiny, about one-sixteenth of an inch long.

Years later, I had the seashells identified as a kind of pebble snail or *Fluminicola*. There were also a few ram's horn snails, freshwater pea clam shells, and beige-colored pond snail shells with much larger spirals.

One morning, I absentmindedly scooped some dirt and uncovered a scorpion. I jumped up and shrieked, "Look, a scorpion!"

People came running over and huddled around me. Squatting down in front of the critter, I touched him with a stick.

"Look, he's raising his tail again," I said. "He's ready to sting me. We'd all better be careful after this."

Everyone nodded as we all silently continued to look at the creature. Soon, they lost interest and drifted back to where they had been searching. I continued to watch the scorpion and silently touched his tan colored body with a stick. Once more his tail shot up. This time he turned his body so his stinger pointed at the stick. Eventually, he retreated into the loose dirt nearby lowering his tail to conceal where he had gone.

~ ⊚ ~

There were thousands of people at Tule Lake Internment Camp and most of us were bored. The lack of meaningful activities was distressing. The government did not provide money for any recreational or adult education programs.

Community leaders recognized what was going on and came up with a plan that included sports, barracks gardens, art classes, and a variety of educational programs to positively stimulate people. The goal was to provide interesting, constructive activities for everyone. The community also wanted to discourage juvenile delinquency, which was no small job for the nearly 19,000 internees imprisoned at Tule Lake.

Volunteers organized all sorts of classes and activities. Because most of us had so little money, we pooled what we could contribute and established a nonprofit cooperative store.

That made it possible for us to buy needed supplies for the various classes.

Almost any kind of class could be set up providing there was a need and a Japanese instructor available to teach it. Volunteers formed clubs to put on public dances in mess halls and develop community entertainment using local talent. They also provided movie nights every so often. I paid ten cents each time to help pay for the rental of the films and to purchase projectors.

For the athletically inclined, Japanese coaches established numerous tournaments for baseball, softball, tennis, track, ping pong, judo, and sumo wrestling. There were teams for men and women, and there were always enthusiastic supporters.

One of the biggest changes was the founding of *The Tulean Dispatch*, the camp's daily newspaper, published in both English and Japanese. The internees wrote, printed, and distributed the paper, which included the daily schedule of activities and classes. I looked forward to reading the paper every day because it gave me a sense of what was going on both in the camp and outside. Most everyone felt more connected because of the camp newspaper, especially because it had folksy articles about various people in the camp.

Another important development announced in *The Tulean Dispatch* was the establishment of church services for the internees. There were Buddhist Sunday School classes for the children and adult Sunday services. Although people came from all Protestant denominations, there was only one Tule Lake Union Church. It provided church services for adults, a high school fellowship, and Christian Youth Fellowship meetings.

In addition to conducting multiple services for the large population, the ministers or priests provided critical counseling for both young and old. Many of us struggled with the complexities of life in what was essentially a prison camp. It would be in this setting that I would later meet a woman who would significantly influence my life.

~⊙~

As our supply of shells increased, we saw information in *The Tulean Dispatch* of various craft classes offered in different places around camp. Amy Nagata, a girl from our ward, joined Mama-san and me and we began going to one of those classes. A young woman named Chiyoko from California was one of our teachers. She seemed to have many ideas of what to do with the shells.

One of Mary's creations from Tule Lake shells, strung together with dental floss she bought at the camp's cooperative store.
PHOTO: RAY GRUENEWALD

She told us to buy some bleach at the canteen and bleach the white shells. We left the tan shells alone. We also bought dental floss, a thimble, and the thinnest needles we could get.

At our first lesson, Chiyoko took one of the needles and threaded it with a long piece of dental floss. Putting a thimble on the middle finger of her right hand, she began to string each shell. I took over from there and made a long strand. I tied the ends of the floss together and was delighted to have made a single stranded necklace. By lining up several strands and twisting them together, I had made a multi-stranded necklace. I was very pleased with the results.

Over time, some of the women made stunning seashell necklaces, seashell **corsage**s, and other art pieces from their found shells. I made several necklaces and learned to make other things, too. I went back to the cooperative canteen and bought fingernail polish and other kinds of paint to brighten up the brooches and pins I made. With just a few pointers from Chiyoko, I made flowers, brace-lets, elaborate wall hangings, and many other original decorations.

Mama-san, Amy, and I had fun working together making pretty things. In time, I began to feel calmer, more content with myself. I made gifts for my former classmates and friends at the Vashon Methodist Church. I sent these gifts along with letters. This was my way of staying connected with the outside world.

As I worked beside Mama-san during those quiet days, I reflected on what life had become. *Instead of being at home on Vashon working or making plans to finish high school and go on to college, here I am stringing these tiny shells, one by one, and forming a necklace to hang around my neck.*

It was as though I was piercing each experience, one by one, to form a necklace of memories. Years later, the shells from Tule Lake would be one of my only mementos from my time in intern-ment camps.

~CHAPTER THIRTEEN~

SHARING STORIES

I wanted to be free.

In spite of the positive changes that had started to take place in my daily life, I still longed for my life on Vashon. It was always hardest at night when I was alone with my thoughts. Listening to the night sounds that had become so familiar, I often tossed in bed, unable to sleep, my stomach aching and my feet cold.

Shame and anger kept crowding in as my family faced the daily indignities of being imprisoned. I was now convinced, *America will never accept me as a full-fledged American.*

More and more I felt as if I were in prison. We had a hospital, post office, warehouse, offices, and schools, but it was all surrounded by a barbed-wire fence and guard towers. The only way out was through the guarded main entrance.

There was no place to be alone or to have a private conversation with anyone. Tule Lake internment camp's population peaked at 18,789 Japanese-Americans. The heat, the freezing cold, and the invasive dust storms told me that America had found a special hell for us.

The injustice of it all haunted me. The U.S. government had declared me guilty without giving me a chance to prove I had been a loyal and patriotic citizen.

I often wondered how my parents viewed our situation. Whatever they felt, I never heard them complain to each other or to anyone else. Wherever they walked they did so with erect postures, or they sat with others, listening sympathetically to their complaints. The only thing I was certain about with my parents was their inner strength, their sensitivity to others' points of view, and their love for our family.

I suspected a great deal of their sensibility and detachment from our distressful situation came from the way they grew up in Wakayama-ken, near Osaka, Japan. Mama-san told me that children were almost universally prized in Japan, just as the elderly were. Much attention was given to them as they grew up, and discipline was gently and carefully provided to help the youngsters become mature and productive people.

Mama-san's parents died when she was young, so her brothers and sisters had great pity for their youngest sister and cared tenderly for her. Although girls were often confined to their home or immediate neighborhood, my mother went to a school in another city far beyond where girls of that time normally went. Mama-san's education, especially in history, and her exposure to different parts of Japan set her apart from other Japanese girls in the early 1900s.

I wondered what Mama-san would have done with her life if she had remained in Japan. There were limited opportunities for women in Japan at that time. Society and tradition would have dictated how she lived her life, limiting her choices.

Instead, Mama-san faced a different set of obstacles in America— racism and the language barrier. She was drawn to the United States by the promise of a better life for herself and her family and by her own sense of adventure.

I often wondered what Mama-san's life would have been like if she had been born later when women had more life choices.

Perhaps she might have become a social activist on behalf of the poor or worked for women's rights. She might have had her own business or become a prominent professor in an esteemed university. Perhaps my mother might have had her own car, her own apartment, and her own executive job in a major corporation. But she never spoke about those possibilities, and never did I hear her complain about any of life's circumstances.

She would view the harsh reality of our current life in an internment camp from the perspective of some one who had a larger-than-life view. Even in the darkest days, Mama-san always found something to be grateful for.

People often walked the perimeters of camp for exercise as well as to fight boredom. Manazanar, 1943.

⊰◉⊱

One day, when Amy and I were out taking a walk, we started talking about the kids from California. "We may all be *Niseis*," I said, "but it's like the kids from California are from another world. They're rowdy and use a lot of slang. I'm not used to that."

Amy giggled. "Have you seen the **zoot suits** those guys wear? The big baggy pants with suspenders and the huge jacket! I can't believe they have the nerve to dress like that." She hesitated, then added, "But it's kind of neat, don't you think?"

I laughed. "Maybe, but you'll never get me to dance the **jitterbug** to that loud music like they do—jumping all around, doing the splits, somersaults, and twirling!"

To me, the Japanese Americans from California seemed unruly and overconfident. It may have been my imagination but I thought they looked darker and taller than us, too. I figured it was from all the sunshine in California.

One Sunday, I met a girl from California named Michi. We sat next to each other during one of the church services and started chatting afterward. As we compared notes, I was interested to learn we had similar childhoods, even though she was from California and I was from Washington.

"We got some neighbors to promise to take care of our farm. I'm hoping we can go back there when this is all over," Michi explained. I understood what she was talking about and shared my family's situation.

Michi became quite animated when she talked about her cousin. "I'm really worried about my cousin, Emi, and especially my Uncle George. He was a fisherman and lived on Terminal Island."

"Where is that?"

"It's in Los Angeles," Michi explained, "near the Long Beach Naval Station. That's probably what got the government nervous about the Japanese living there."

"We had a similar situation with some Japanese living on Bainbridge Island in Puget Sound, which is near the Bremerton Naval Base," I explained. "They were the first group to be evacuated from the Puget Sound area."

Michi nodded. "The FBI picked up Uncle George right after Pearl Harbor because he had been a leader in the Japanese community for years. All the other *Issei* men with fishing licenses

Fear and hatred of the Japanese became widespread, especially in California, after the bombing of Pearl Harbor. Japanese Americans who were also citizens of the U.S. were shunned and forced out of their neighborhoods.

were rounded up and jailed, too."

"All the other men, too? Wow, that sounds like a lot of men," I responded. "The only man from Vashon who was picked up was the president of our Japanese association. I was really scared they would come for my father because he was the secretary for so many years."

Michi then explained how the government gave all the Japanese American families on Terminal Island only 48 hours to get out of their homes to leave for the internment camps. "Most of the fathers were already jailed," Michi said, "so the mothers didn't even have time to buy suitcases or anything. Can you just imagine the panic?"

Frustration and anger clouded Michi's pretty face. I found it hard to find words to comfort her. "That's outrageous!" I agreed. "We only had eight days, but at least we knew what was coming."

"These families had to leave practically everything: their boats, their homes, everything they had worked for over a lifetime," added Michi, shaking her head. "And it gets worse. In the midst of the crisis, some *hakujins* (white men) showed up with their trucks. They offered to buy furniture and stuff from these families for pennies! My aunt was so desperate, she sold these vultures her dining room set and all of her appliances for only forty dollars!"

Michi's eyes flashed in anger. "I mean, what was she supposed to do? My aunt didn't know what to prepare for, and she might have needed cash just to eat, for all she knew. Besides, if she left that stuff in the house, someone might just have taken it anyway."

This conversation really opened my eyes. Now, I understood why the Californians were so angry. I would be, too, if I had been treated that way.

I told Michi about some of my family's desperate efforts around that same time. When we realized we were going to be forced to evacuate, the Vashon Japanese-American Club sent a scout to see if we could voluntarily relocate to an area in Idaho. However, our scout reported that the people in Idaho were unwilling to lease, rent, or sell any land to *any* Japanese.

Even the local Japanese Americans in Idaho didn't want us— and with good reason. The Idaho governor indicated that he was considering having the evacuation orders extended to include his state should any out-of-state Japanese try to make a home there.

"We were not welcomed on the coast and we were not welcomed inland," I told Michi.

Michi and I sat in silence for a long time. I stared at the rows of barracks and thought about the thousands of us struggling to find meaning in the things happening to us. Countless times I asked myself, *"Why?"* There were no answers.

~CHAPTER FOURTEEN~

MAKING FRIENDS

Slowly, I began to come out of my shell and focus on what was going on around me.

When I wasn't in classes or working in the mess hall, I began helping in a variety of places. I started in the physical education program for grade school children. I liked being with the little kids, cheering them on, giving them tips on how to hold a bat or hit the ball.

I also helped in classes for the kids with poor eyesight by reading to many of the students. This school was named for Helen Keller. Helping these children made me realize I still had many things to be thankful for, including my eyesight. These extra activities helped me to gradually open up and recognize lots of changes going on.

I could see the traditional Japanese ways were changing as the children became more Americanized. Many of the children did not want to eat with their families or stay close to their parents. Instead, they became more independent and often disobeyed their parents.

The young people were rebelling and there didn't seem to be much that could be done about it. I felt myself being tugged in so many directions. On top of all the confusing feelings of being a teenager caught between two cultures, I was also a prisoner in the internment camp and my normal life was on hold.

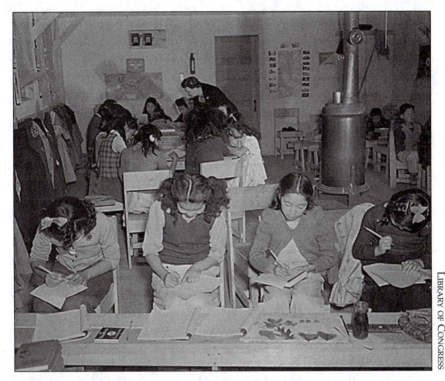

Students in grammar school classroom at Tule Lake, 1943.

Some teenage boys and girls began walking through the camp openly holding hands with each other. Some girls wore very short skirts and tee shirts, a popular style during World War II. Jitterbugging to loud music became a common occurrence in the recreation halls. Established Japanese traditions were unraveling. Mama-san didn't say much, but I'm sure she observed these changes and was disturbed.

At seventeen years old, I watched these changes from a distance. I was curious, but I was not ready to join in—not yet.

One day as I was cleaning up in the mess hall, a man about twenty-five-years old approached me and asked, "Do you know how to play card games?"

"No, I don't."

"Would you like to learn how?"

I thought a minute. Playing cards was one of the **taboos** in our family. It ranked with smoking, drinking, gambling, and dancing as behaviors we were supposed to stay away from.

Remembering that, I said, "I'm not supposed to do that."

"What's wrong with playing a little card game?" the young man persisted.

"I don't know. I suppose my folks consider it the same as gambling."

He reassured me there was no betting involved and the card game was just for fun. His name was Richard and he seemed nice enough.

Boy, I could sure use a little fun right now, I thought. *Maybe it wouldn't hurt to try it a little bit.*

"I guess I could try it," I responded hesitantly.

Richard and I agreed to meet at my family's place a short time later. When I told Mama-san, she lowered her head and looked at me hesitantly. I could tell that she was not pleased, but she didn't say anything.

Up until this time, I had never had a date with a boy. On Vashon the Japanese teenagers didn't date or go to dances at all. They might have done that in the urban areas like Seattle, but in the country, dating came much later.

Richard came over a few times and we played different kinds of card games. My parents were polite, but didn't approve. One night, not long after we started playing cards, Richard asked me to go dancing with him. Although jitterbugging was the rage, I did not know how to do it. I watched the kids whirling and swinging and laughing like they were having a great time. However, the adults complained about the loud music and how the kids "just jump all over the place." It looked like fun to me, but I was hesitant about going.

I told Richard I didn't know how to jitterbug, but he persisted and was convincing. When I asked Mama-san, she quietly expressed her concerns. She did not approve of the wild dancing, and she did not want me to go with Richard because he was a divorced man.

I didn't like hearing what Mama-san had to say. I could feel the resistance building inside of me. Even though I didn't want to disappoint Mama-san, I felt like I just had to break out of the mold I was in.

Speaking louder than I intended, I blurted out, "I want to go and I am going." Without looking back, I left the apartment.

There were quite a few young people already at the mess hall when Richard and I arrived. I had mixed feelings of excitement and reservation. After awhile, a lot of couples got up and started dancing. Richard offered his hand and I took it.

We bobbed around to the beat of the music, but I felt like I had two left feet. I kept looking at Richard as he twisted and turned and rocked back and forth. I tried to keep up, but I felt stiff as a board.

The music finally ended, and I was relieved. When Richard looked the other way, I ran back home, defeated and embarrassed. I crept back into the apartment and didn't look at Mama-san or say a word. I had to admit to myself, *I don't fit into that crowd, but where do I fit?*

I never went to another dance throughout our internment camp days, but I always wished I could have learned to dance.

In the midst of these conflicts, I thought about my mother's favorite concept of *on*—the Japanese sense of obligation to family, and a debt of gratitude and respect for each member of the family. It had always been a part of our lives at home and here in camp it was being tested by the changes taking place all around us. I had to figure out how much tradition I wanted to keep in my life.

◁◉◁

Sharing conversations with other people at the camp helped me. I began to understand that many Japanese-American families had a far worse situation than my family. Our neighbors on Vashon never

turned against us, and we never experienced the daily discrimination so many Japanese Americans felt, especially in California.

Eighty percent of the Japanese population on the West Coast
lived in California. Most Japanese were highly productive, successful people in whatever work they pursued. As a result, they became
the target of some white people's fears, envy, and prejudice.

In the years leading up to World War II, there were laws enacted
to keep more Japanese from coming to the United States. There
were also laws that kept Japanese Americans from owning land or
becoming too successful in their new lives in America.

World War II provided the excuse for removing the Japanese
Americans on the West Coast and to eliminate business **competi-
tion**. As a result of the evacuation, many Japanese Americans lost
their land, homes, and whatever business gains they had made.

When I realized what extraordinary sacrifices the first-genera-
tion Japanese had gone through, this made me profoundly sad and
angry. I scolded myself, *How protected I have been and how hard my
judgment was of the Japanese I called "those Californians."*

Learning about the experiences of Japanese in California led
me to realize that even though I was still held against my will in
a camp, I was better off than they were. I felt guilty. One day, I
finally decided, *Snap out of it and quit feeling so sorry for yourself!*

⩗◉⩗

The *Tulean Dispatch* was now a well-established part of camp life.
My parents enjoyed reading the news in Japanese, and Yoneichi and
I pored through the English section. I always read the sermon titles
for the church services, and I attended church regularly.

At the close of church services on a warm October day, I met a
surprise visitor, a Caucasian woman named Zola Lenz. She was 45
years old, tall, and heavy-set with graying brown hair and clear
hazel eyes. She wore a lightweight tweed suit and sensible shoes.
Zola was a housewife from Hicksville, Ohio, and she was Methodist.

Zola approached me with her hand outstretched, interested in learning more about the internment camps. She was on vacation for a few weeks and had met our pastor, Reverend Yasui. He suggested Zola attend the internment camp service.

After exchanging greetings, we found a couple of chairs off to the side of the room where the service had been held. I told her where I was from and then asked, "What do you want to know?"

As we began to share our stories, I wondered how I had become so much more bold and worldly. There I was, talking with a stranger about my life without asking my parents' permission. Zola wanted to learn about my family's history and what happened that we ended up in an internment camp.

Young people attend Sunday school class. Manzanar 1943.

"Okay," I said. Then, I took a deep breath, thinking, *What could I say to make this white woman understand how deeply shaken my world has become?* I wanted her to know about our family—our dignity, our history, and our uniqueness. We were not spies for the

Japanese Emperor, nor were we faceless, yellow-bellied soldiers as portrayed in newspapers and magazines.

I told her about my father being the fourth of five sons in a farming family in Wakayama-ken, Japan. He was the adventurer and traveled to the United States in 1898 when he was 21, looking for work. In 1922, he returned to Japan and married my mother, Mitsuno Horiye. Together, they settled on Vashon Island to work on their ten-acre berry farm and raise a family. Yoneichi was born in 1923 and I was born in 1925.

I also told Zola about the prejudice my parents faced in America because they were Japanese. They couldn't become citizens, they couldn't vote, and they couldn't own land.

Shaking her head, Zola lamented, "It's not right that some people could become citizens and others couldn't just because of racial backgrounds. We're all from immigrant families. My ancestors came from Russia."

Hearing Zola's sympathy made me feel great. She was the first white person to hear my story since the evacuation and I felt affirmed and supported. Plus, I felt so knowledgeable as I talked with Zola.

At one point, Zola asked, "You've used the terms *Issei* and *Nisei*. What do they mean?"

"The *Isseis* are people like my parents who were born in Japan, came to this country, and became the first generation of Japanese in America. Those of us born here, like my brother and me, are called *Niseis*, the second generation in America.

"Although *Isseis* have lived in America for decades, they kept many of the values and customs of Japan," I continued. "The *Niseis*, like myself, were born and raised here and are thoroughly Americanized."

"Oh, yes, the typical immigrant experience," Zola nodded, understanding the situation. "So there could be a cultural gap within the family?"

"Yes," I replied. "There can be if parents and children don't talk and share with each other. That's happening in some families now."

Zola and I shifted in our seats. The folding metal chairs were hard and uncomfortable. She seemed interested, so I continued, although I thought, *Mama-san will be wondering where I am.* But this conversation was too important. Suddenly, at 17, I was an expert in something with ideas worth hearing.

Then Zola asked about the evacuation of all Japanese Americans from the West Coast. She was from Ohio and many people in other parts of the United States knew very little about our plight.

"This whole evacuation process has been just awful," I admitted honestly. "The attack on Pearl Harbor turned our world completely upside down. I couldn't believe this could happen to us, especially because we are citizens—but here we are."

"What bothers you most about living in this camp?" Zola asked with great interest.

"Well, there are a number of things—the boring food, the dust storms, the heat and the cold in these flimsy barracks. A big one is the lack of space—so many of us crammed into such tight quarters—there is no privacy."

After a moment's reflection, I added, "I think the biggest problem is the bitterness simmering among a lot of people in all the camps over being evacuated and our having to live in these kinds of places."

Zola brought both hands up to her mouth. Her eyes widened. "What will you and your family do? Is there anything I can do to help you?"

I wasn't sure what to tell Zola. I did reassure her that my family's strength helped me a lot. "Every day we come together and share what we saw and heard that day. It's hard to know where all of this is going," I concluded, " but we will have to deal with it as it happens."

When Zola stood up to leave, she shook my hand and said, "Will you write and keep me informed? I want to stay in touch with you. I would also like to share your story with my friends. Most people in the Midwest don't have any idea what's going on."

Taking her hand in both of mine, I felt touched and honored by her interest and concern. I said, "Thanks for listening. This has helped me a lot, too."

Zola turned and waved as she left the church. I thought, *Not all white Americans hate us.*

Not long after our visit, Zola sent me a letter. We began exchanging letters regularly. Her letters were always encouraging and she repeatedly expressed appreciation for all that I had shared with her.

Zola came into my life at an important time when I felt isolated and rejected by my country, and confused about my identity. I desperately needed someone from the outside to understand and accept my pain, and acknowledge that I had a right to my feelings.

Zola heard me. Because of her, I put Ohio on my secret list of states I wanted to move to once I was freed from the internment camp. Emotionally, I felt my heart flowering and turning toward the sun.

≺ CHAPTER FIFTEEN ≻

FREEDOM

At last, the armed soldiers, the invading search lights, and the closed gates were gone. What a relief!

After months of being watched by soldiers with guns, it was almost a shock to see the gates of the internment camp open. No more soldiers closely watching us from the watchtowers, and no more military authority controlling who could leave the internment camp. If we wished, we could freely walk right through the front gates of the camp to explore the surrounding areas without having to ask for permission.

The government's War Relocation Authority (WRA), a civilian authority, was now managing the internment camps. Initially, the U.S. Army was responsible for moving Japanese Americans from their homes to the assembly centers and then to relocation centers. Now, the WRA handled the day-to-day operation of the internment camps. When the change finally happened around October 1942, the most dramatic difference was the removal of the Army guards from the watchtowers.

With this new freedom, I decided to go beyond the barbed-wire fence. I wanted to hike up to Castle Rock in the hills surrounding Tule Lake camp. Every day hundreds of people walked outside the fenced camp and climbed the hillside. I wanted to go, too. My friend, Amy, agreed to join me.

When we stepped outside the barbed-wire fence, we stopped, looked at each other, and took a deep breath. We raised our arms and shouted, "We're free!" Compared to what we had been through, this really felt free—at least, for the moment.

After a couple hours climbing up a winding pathway around boulders, sagebrush, and dried grass, we came to a natural resting place. Leaning against some big boulders, we looked back at the huge camp. I could see my block, 74, and I could see my barrack, 7404. A high fence surrounded the entire camp with barbed wire along the top.

From that altitude we could see everywhere. There was a light haze over the barracks below, but in the hills the air was pleasantly warm and clear. *I am free! I am transformed!* I thought. Then I imagined myself flying away, soaring all over the United States even though I had never been to any of the places I imagined—the Rocky Mountains, Yellowstone National Park, Chicago, Washington D.C., New Orleans, and the Grand Canyon.

Then I started flying north along the Pacific coastline toward my home. Once I was back on my farm on Vashon, I stuffed my mouth full of sweet, sun-ripened strawberries. I glided over the pond on our makeshift raft and flopped down on the lush green lawn to rest in the sunshine. I listened to the happy birds singing nearby and watched the clouds floating lazily across the blue sky. Finally, I imagined myself falling into a quiet, peaceful sleep in my own bed in our own home.

My fantasy was interrupted when I heard a strange voice exclaim, "Well, this is more like it."

A girl had come around the bend. She stood looking back at the camp. "A grand view of the ugliest place on Earth," she said without a trace of humor.

I sat up and shaded my eyes to get a better look at who was talking. She was tall, slender, and about our age. Bold, scarlet lipstick carefully outlined her lips, just like the actresses in the movies. She wore tight, black slacks and a short sleeve, black shirt opened down to the fourth button. Something inside of me recoiled at her appearance and the sullen look on her face.

"Hi," Amy responded. Then she got the courage to ask, "Who are you?"

"I'm Mary Otani from Sacramento. And you two?" I could hear arrogance in her voice.

"I'm Amy Nagata from Tacoma, Washington, and this is my friend, Mary Matsuda from Vashon Island near Seattle."

"Hi. It's a nice day for a hike, isn't it?" I commented, trying to sound polite.

"Yeah, but even one day here is one day too many," she said heatedly.

Amy replied, "I don't like it any better than you do, but I'm not sure what we can do about it now."

"At least we're outside the barbed-wire fence right now," I said and shrugged my shoulders. "Maybe this is the first of more freedom to come. We can hope so, don't you think?"

"Well, maybe," Mary replied, "but I'm not going to hold my breath. I'm sick of the government. They came and took away my dad right after Pearl Harbor, and we still don't know where he is. We've probably lost our farm by this time, too."

Her voice faltered. She turned her head sadly and stared off in the distance.

My heart sank. I thought, *She still doesn't know where her father is? No wonder she's so angry.*

"I'm terribly sorry," I said softly.

Mary sat down beside us and told us about her family's experience after Pearl Harbor; her father's disappearance, the FBI raid on their home, the difficulty trying to save their farm, and the evacuation. Hers was only a slight variation on a story very familiar to us. All I could do was nod my head in acknowledgment, but my heart cried out at her pain and bitterness—which was worse than mine.

After a time, it started to get fairly hot, so we decided to walk back to camp together. We walked single file down the path, each of us caught up in our own thoughts.

At the entrance into camp I turned to Mary, put my hand on her shoulder and said softly, "I wish there was something I could do for you."

"No, there's nothing," she responded. "But thank you for listening and understanding."

"I hope your dad gets released and joins your family real soon," I added, before going my own way.

If I had been in her shoes and my father had been taken away, I would have been devastated. There seemed to be nothing more I could say or do.

~ ⑥ ~

Tension gradually began to increase around camp. Groups of boys, mostly from California, were restless and openly bitter about the evacuation and continued confinement. They began roaming the camp, looking threatening. The traditional discipline and the moral code of the Japanese family were disintegrating. Now, angry young men began to harass people confined at the camp.

One day, when my brother and I came out of a church service, a group of boys from California made nasty remarks about us "people from the north." Before Yoneichi and I headed for home, I saw one of the boys "accidentally" bump into a boy from Vashon and apologize profusely as if mocking the Japanese way. He and his friends took off laughing loudly about the importance of being "polite."

After that interaction, I was afraid to go to church alone. Yoneichi and I decided to get together with other young people from our end of the camp and go as a group to church services. Before we left, the boys put the girls in the middle, and we proceeded to the services held in the central part of camp.

We joined some people we knew from the southeastern part of camp, the area we called "Alaska" because they were physically separated from the rest of the camp by an irrigation ditch. They, too, were from the Pacific Northwest. We would meet outside of the barrack where the service was held, and we all walked in together.

Reverend Matsui, our Protestant minister, was a **bespectacled** man who looked tall and slim in his long, black clerical clothing. He could see the problems threatening family life at the internment camp. He urged families to investigate applying for permanent leave and to move out of the camp. Several things took place that made these opportunities possible.

President Roosevelt appointed Dillon S. Myer to head up the WRA in June 1942. Shortly after Myer took over, a WRA top aide advised him that long-term confinement of the evacuees was not a good idea and that internees should be resettled as quickly as possible. Myer made an inspection tour himself and came to the same conclusion.

Temporary leave opportunities became available for people in the internment camps. Labor shortages on farms required the use of Japanese-American workers, even on some farms in the West.

A small group of educators, plus YMCA/YWCA officials from the San Francisco Bay area, and even California Governor Culbert Olson expressed concern for the Japanese-American students whose college education had been disrupted by the evacuation.

In May 1942, the National Student Relocation Council was organized in Chicago. By that fall, many Japanese-American students were cleared by the FBI to leave for the Midwest and East to continue their education. However, Japanese-American students could not return to schools on the West Coast.

If you did not have a criminal record or a reputation for disloyal acts, camp administrators decided you could qualify to leave. However, no one could return home to any West Coast state.

We could leave but we couldn't go home. *What choice was that?* I wondered.

Reverend Matsui's open, self-confident manner conveyed a sense of strength and personal power to those who looked to him for direction. For those who disagreed with him, he evoked fear and anger.

Reverend Matsui made numerous trips to various cities in the Midwest and East Coast to evaluate how the *Niseis* who had moved to the "outside" were getting along. He provided us with valuable information on how to make successful transitions "out there" where the climate was more normal. Reverend Matsui's reports encouraged some Japanese to request permission to leave and to re-establish themselves and their families in parts of America far from the West Coast.

I wondered, *Is there another reason why we are encouraged to leave camp? Could it be that by now we have become an economic burden on the country?*

The war seemed to drag on and on. Japan was the enemy, and so there was no end in sight as to how long the U.S. government would have to pay to keep internment camps open.

While getting out of the internment camp sounded great, realistically, there were many obstacles. Japanese Americans had to have a sponsor—someone who would take care of their initial needs, especially housing, food, and employment, once they arrived at a chosen location. Few Americans were willing to sponsor Japanese American families because there was a wartime hatred of Japan and anything Japanese. However, there were a few courageous groups such as the Quakers and some Christian churches that offered to help.

Before we could get clearance to leave, camp officials had to approve our request by making criminal background checks and reviewing evidence of "loyal citizenship." Those who were among the first to leave camp realized they would be carefully watched. They would be regarded as examples of typical Japanese-American evacuees. So, they had to be on their best behavior.

By and large, Japanese-American students whose college education had been interrupted by the war were the first ones who took advantage of the leave policy. Most had to transfer to different colleges, but at least they could continue studying. However, the churches and the government were unsuccessful in getting large numbers of evacuees to leave the camps. This fact did not go unnoticed by the WRA.

∴ ⑥ ∾

After six months in the camp, I was slowly emerging from my depressed state. Life seemed to gallop ahead, while at the same time stand still. Many things were happening: I was developing

High school recess at Manzanar Internment Camp, 1943.

ANSEL ADAMS, LIBRARY OF CONGRESS

different skills, gradually making some friends, observing changes in the administration of the camp, and experiencing a measure of freedom that those shifts brought.

Finishing high school and learning to make do with what was available became high priorities. Changes were taking place in many family relationships, and I noticed how much stronger my own family was.

Some families at the internment camp considered relocating to Japan, but this did not become an option until much later. My parents never considered this option, nor did I. Before they left Japan they had made a commitment to make their home in the United States.

I could not see a clear direction for my life. There was a tug to leave the camp behind and venture into a new life on the outside after I graduated from high school. But I realized once I left camp, there would be no coming back.

I often worried, *What would happen to my parents?* The powerful feeling of *on*—loyalty to family—caused me to pause and reflect, *What might be the best thing for all of us, not just for myself?*

Still shell-shocked from the sudden, bitter disruption of my life, I couldn't imagine building a life in a different part of the country where I would be a visible and possibly a hated minority. I was not yet ready to venture out alone. However, events would soon take place that would influence me to change my mind.

CHAPTER SIXTEEN

NO NO OR YES YES?

Yoneichi burst through the door and the three of us looked up in alarm.

"Hey!" he said grimly, "the guys are saying there was a big riot at Manzanar yesterday. Somebody even got killed."

The three of us gasped, then we all bombarded Yoneichi with questions. Everywhere in camp people were talking about the riot at Manzanar Internment Camp in central California. In the laundry room, women spoke in hushed voices. Outside, groups of young men held loud debates on the possibility of more rioting, **martial law**, and what the government should do. Rumors spread like wildfire.

Most people were visibly afraid. A few seemed excited, even energized by having something to break the boredom of every-day life in the camp. This riot took place exactly one year after the bombing of Pearl Harbor.

I heard rumors of conflicts between groups of people, of shady deals that drove people to the point of explosive action, and of general distrust of the camp administration. Meanwhile, official communications from government representatives about the riot were matter-of-fact, soothing, and not informative. I spent long hours reading the reports in the *Tulean Dispatch*. Then I wondered what was not included in the stories.

Yoneichi told us he thought there was more disruption to come. "There could be trouble here, too," he warned. "I think it's best for us to keep a low profile. We don't want to become targets."

We would later learn that primarily two converging factors caused the Manzanar riots. One was the general social unrest due to the brutal evacuation, forced confinement, poor living conditions, and lack of meaningful work, among other camp life problems. Manzanar held all of the Japanese Americans forced to evacuate from Terminal Island in Southern California. Their evacuation had been particularly cruel and their bitterness was understandable.

The other factor was some Manzanar internees were members of a pro-American group, the Japanese American Citizen League (JACL). Throughout the internment crisis, the JACL conducted well-intentioned but sometimes secret work that the JACL thought would be helpful to all Japanese Americans. However, some internees were highly suspicious of JACL members who, at times, met secretly with government officials and provided information and made recommendations.

At Manzanar, some internees claimed JACL members were providing the camp administration with the names of so-called "troublemakers." This made other internees angry and suspicious. All of the internment camps to some extent were polarized into two groups—the pro-American groups versus those who were not.

The news of the Manzanar riot and army troops shooting dead two Japanese Americans shocked me. Fear became my overriding emotion. *Something is terribly wrong,* I thought. *Could the violence spread to Tule Lake?*

All of this reminded me of how I felt the year before when we got the disturbing news about Pearl Harbor. I knew instinctively it was the beginning of something that would soon overtake my life, but I didn't know where it might lead, and it was beyond my control.

In addition to Manzanar, there were strikes and protests at other internment camps. In general, there was growing unrest in all the camps. I had a feeling that something threatening was about to take place at Tule Lake camp. Perhaps there would be riots or something even worse. People seemed ready for trouble.

≈◉≈

Manzanar Internment Camp street scene.

The Manzanar riots created a crisis for the WRA, which was already aware of the tensions building in the internment camps. The government decided it needed to find a way to separate those Japanese who were pro-America from those Japanese who were not. The government reasoned that if this wasn't done, and done quickly, there would be more violence.

The WRA was working on a plan for mass registration of all adults to determine who qualified for school or employment outside of the camps. The WRA wanted to return internees to a normal life as quickly as possible, but only those whom they decided could be "trusted." The government wanted a systematic way to determine and document who would not be a threat to the United States outside of the internment camps.

Separately, in January 1943 Secretary of War Henry L. Stimson announced the formation of a military combat team made up of Japanese-American men from the internment camps and the Hawaiian Islands. These young men would be sent to fight in World War II. One critical piece of information the Army needed to know was whether these young men would be loyal to the United States.

When the WRA learned about the Army's plans, they decided to combine the two projects and accomplish both tasks with a questionnaire. The government officials thought this was a good idea, but the results in the Japanese-American internment camps were disastrous.

We knew to expect this questionnaire from the government because the *Tulean Dispatch* published an explanation provided by the camp administration. We were hopeful that this questionnaire would help bring an end to the conflict.

One day, our block manager made an announcement at breakfast that the head of each family should come to the manager's office to pick up questionnaires for each family member who was seventeen years and older. Authorities hoped the questionnaires would be completed and returned within ten days.

Papa-san brought the questionnaires back for each of us and we sat down promptly to read and fill them out. The majority of the questions were simple. They covered topics such as education, previous employment, knowledge of the Japanese language, number of relatives in Japan, foreign investments and travel, religious and organizational affiliations, sports interests, hobbies, magazines and newspapers customarily read, and possession of dual citizenship.

But there were two questions with two variations that were anything but simple. Ultimately, these two questions would tear apart the Japanese-American community and even individual families.

As a young man capable of serving in the war, Yoneichi's form read like this:

Question 27. Are you willing to serve in the armed
forces of the United States on combat
duty, wherever ordered?

Question 28. Will you swear unqualified allegiance
to the United States of America and
faithfully defend the United States
from any or all attack by foreign
or domestic forces, and forswear any
form of allegiance or obedience to
the Japanese emperor, to any other
foreign government, power or organization?

My form, and those of my immigrant parents, read like this:

For Isseis of both sexes and all female Nisei over
seventeen years of age:

Question 27. If the opportunity presents itself
and you are found qualified, would
you be willing to volunteer for the
Army Nurse Corps or WAAC [Women's
Auxiliary Army Corps]?

Question 28. Will you swear unqualified allegiance
to the United States of America and
forswear any form of allegiance or
obedience to the Japanese emperor, or
any other foreign government, power
or organization?

As I read and reread the questions, the hair on the back of my
neck rose. I was caught between outrage and fear.

Do I really want to go into the Army Nurse Corps or the WAAC? I asked myself. Worse, Yoneichi was being forced to choose between an unknown, presumably horrible penalty from the government or join the military with the possibility of death on foreign soil.

Question 28 seemed even more mysterious and troubling. I thought, *I am an American citizen, why would I have any allegiance to the Japanese emperor? Why are they asking me that question?* It was confusing. I didn't get it.

What did these questions mean to Papa-san and Mama-san, especially since there were laws that forbade them from being U.S. citizens? These seemed like trick questions. I began questioning the government's motives.

The questionnaire seemed to throw everyone off balance. My family was unusually quiet for nearly two days. We were shocked by the sudden demand to declare our intentions. We also wondered about the consequences of our choices.

Everyone around us seemed confused, too. People had different interpretations of what the questions meant. The noise level in the mess hall, in the bathroom, and in the laundry room rose as people began debating the issues. Arguments broke out within families, between friends, and between people from the north (Washington and Oregon) and south (California). I had trouble sleeping at night, hearing angry voices at all hours in our barrack and in neighboring barracks.

Some *Isseis* focused upon the title of their questionnaire: "Application for Leave Clearance."

"If I fill this out," one woman asked, "does that mean I am applying to leave camp? Where would I go? I can't go back to my home on the West Coast."

To others, question 28 sounded like a trick question. Answering "Yes" would imply an admission of allegiance to the Japanese emperor in the past.

⸱⸛⊚⸛⸱

When U.S. Army recruiters arrived at Tule Lake internment camp to get men to register for the military, Yoneichi went to find out what the recruiters had to say. He also wanted to see how the other men at the camp would respond. He came back shaking his head.

"That was some kind of wild meeting," he said. "You should have seen those guys. I thought some of them were about to explode."

"What were they so mad about?" I asked, not understanding their anger.

"Some of them were old military guys who got kicked out of the Army after Pearl Harbor because they're Japanese, but for some reason they are now eligible for the draft again. Others were there just to challenge and harass the recruiters about the questionnaire."

"Did you find out anything useful?" asked Papa-san.

"Yeah, the recruiters said that questions 27 and 28 are a way to determine who has security clearance for military service," explained Yoneichi. "When you put it that way, it seems fairly straightforward, but some of the guys had really good points. One of them said that serving in a segregated unit with only Japanese-American soldiers could put us into the riskiest positions at the whim of military leadership."

Yoneichi explained how some men asked why the Army would establish an all-Japanese military unit. And someone else said he didn't want to serve in the U.S. military because he might possibly have to fight against his brother or cousin in Japan.

Mama-san listened with a worried look on her face.

"Whoever came up with these questions didn't think through what they were asking," Yoneichi said emphatically. "Nor did they consider all the different circumstances people would find themselves in."

Aside from the confusion young men like Yoneichi faced, and other *Niseis* like myself, I wondered about my parents' generation. For elderly *Isseis*, question 27 was ridiculous. How could older men and women who weren't even citizens of the United States possibly qualify for the Women's Army Auxiliary Corps? Those who volunteered for the WAAC would be the first females to serve in the U.S. Army.

WING LUKE MUSEUM

Issei *meeting at Minidoka Internment Camp.*

Question 28 unthinkingly asked the *Isseis* to swear unqualified allegiance to the United States, even though the United States had prevented them from becoming citizens, and now imprisoned them. They were being asked to formally give up any loyalty to Japan and possibly fight against the very country with which they were still citizens. For the aliens to answer "Yes" would mean they would be without a country—neither a citizen of the United States nor Japan.

And what if Japan won the war? The *Isseis* would be traitors if they voted "Yes." But to vote "No" could result in deportation. We all wondered, *What are we supposed to do?*

↙◎↘

There were no simple solutions for anybody. Even those who felt strongly one way or the other had doubts that could not be answered. Previously friendly relationships were disrupted by heated arguments, sometimes leading to verbal threats, shoving, and even violence. The block managers and the camp administration were hopelessly overwhelmed with questions they could not answer. Attempts to have meetings with government officials to discuss the questions and get additional information were denied in our camp.

Gangs of angry young men began to roam the camp, especially in areas where the Northwest families lived. Because many of us from the Northwest had lived more integrated lives with our white neighbors and we had been treated more respectfully during our evacuation, we were more apt to vote "Yes Yes."

Some Californians considered us "**stool pigeons**" or informers. These men posted handwritten signs in both English and Japanese in various public places, warning: "Do not sign 'Yes Yes'" or "Do not fill out the questionnaire." These threats later led to gangs beating up people who did not agree with them.

I had never been so terrified in my life. Suddenly, I was hated by my government and by other Japanese Americans. *Why?* I thought. *Just being from Washington State makes them think my family and I are disloyal to our own kind? This is totally insane.*

Within a week, the Army and the WRA authorities realized their mistake. They quickly made a revision, and postponed the deadline for turning in the questionnaires. The following question directed at the *Isseis* replaced question 28:

```
Will you swear to abide by the laws of the
United States and to take no action which would
in any way interfere with the war effort of the
United States?
```

The revision came too late. The damage had been done. Distrust, confusion, and anger prevailed. Many *Isseis* declared they would answer "No No" in protest to the way the U.S. government had treated them.

The young Japanese-American men who refused to go into the military were labeled "No-No Boys." The most vocal did so out of protest, but there were other reasons. Some of the men took their role as the oldest male in the family very seriously. By tradition, they were responsible for their aging parents and their siblings. Some of these men chose to remain in the internment camps with their families and fight the whole evacuation process.

In their haste to get the registration underway quickly, the government and the WRA had thrust every Japanese-American family onto the horns of a terrible dilemma. In time, this questionnaire would rip families apart, ruin close friendships, and polarize the entire Japanese-American community for a generation. This was clearly not the government's intention.

The process turned out to be a tragic mistake from which some individuals never recovered. As one of my friends said years later, "In all my life, answering those two questions was the hardest thing I have ever done."

᛫◎᛫

Tension continued to escalate as the deadline for the questionnaire approached. After the Manzanar riot, the army had returned to all the camps and soldiers constantly watched us. Whenever I left our apartment, I looked for threatening signals from everyone. I realized the darkest truth of our situation: *We really are vulnerable; the threat to our lives is real.*

While standing near the barbed-wire fence at the edge of camp one day, looking beyond the armed soldiers and guard towers, I looked toward Castle Rock and the darkening sky. I asked no one in particular, *Where is God in all this? Doesn't He care and watch over us?*

CHAPTER SEVENTEEN

THE GREAT DIVIDE

One night around midnight, someone started pounding urgently on our door.

Yoneichi leaped up to open it. Yoneichi's former classmate from Vashon, Bobby, burst in.

"Ken Ishimoto got beat up."

Yoneichi threw on some clothes and disappeared with Bobby into the darkness. We didn't sleep the rest of the night, waiting for Yoneichi to return.

When he came back, Yoneichi told us what happened. "Ken was unconscious on the ground behind his apartment. His mom was beside him, calling his name. There was blood running from his forehead down his face. His clothes were all messed up. Several of us got there about the same time. I lifted Ken's head and spoke to him. He didn't answer."

"He must have been knocked out," I said.

"Yeah. We got a blanket under him and six of us took him to the hospital. About a half hour later Ken woke up."

"Did he know any of the people who beat him up?" Mama-san asked.

"No. They're probably from Sacramento or are *Kibeis* [Japanese-Americans born in the United States but educated in Japan] like most of the 'No-No' guys. I heard Ken talking about signing 'Yes

Yes' and telling other guys to do the same. That's probably why he got beat up."

Mama-san said anxiously, "Yoneichi-san, please be careful."

I looked away, troubled.

≺◎≻

The Loyalty Oath plunged me back into depression. Outrage streamed through my thoughts daily. *How could an 18-year-old girl like me be suspected of sabotaging my country? How dare they question my loyalty?*

One of my Japanese cultural norms was absolute obedience to authority. I was expected to be a model American citizen. Juvenile delinquency or antisocial behavior of any type was unacceptable in our family as well as among most *Isseis* and *Niseis*.

Often, I walked alone around the perimeter of the camp, trying to see clear of my outrage and   with my America. Often, I would meet others walking in pairs, groups, or alone. We were all people with black hair, slanted eyes, and troubled thoughts. We all walked a path of endless questions.

At our school assemblies in the internment camp, I repeated the Pledge of Allegiance daily and sang "America" and "The Star Spangled Banner." I sang, "My country 'tis of thee, Sweet land of liberty." I wondered, *Liberty for whom?*

I pledged, "…One nation, indivisible, with liberty and justice for all." How I longed for that equal justice and freedom!

How I longed for the quiet, tranquil days on the farm. I wanted the simple tasks of preparing the fields to yield the biggest, sweetest berries. How I wanted to sit at dusk on the small hill on our farm where I could gaze at Mount Rainier off to the southeast, situated like a great snowy temple. I thought about the freedom I had enjoyed and taken for granted on Vashon Island—all of that now seemed lost forever.

One night I had a vivid dream that haunted me. In the dream my family and I were among a throng of people gathered for some kind of town meeting. There were sudden blasts from a machine gun. As I whirled in the direction of the shots, I realized with horror that people, including my parents and brother, were starting to fall like a wave as bullets penetrated their bodies. Blood gushed everywhere. Mama-san slowly began to sink with blood spurting from her chest. As I lunged to catch her, I bolted up in bed dripping with sweat, my heart pounding, and my throat so tight I could scarcely breathe. That night after the nightmare, I couldn't stop thinking, *What will become of us?*

◊

A few days after that nightmare I was laying on my cot when Yoneichi came home from work. He hung up his cook's apron on a nail, kicked off his shoes, and flopped on his cot. He looked at ease in his tan slacks and white T-shirt as he laced his fingers behind his head and stretched out. Papa-san mentioned we had been talking about the escalating unrest in the camps.

Yoneichi sat up, swung his legs over the side of the cot and faced us. "Another internee was shot and killed in Manzanar," he said. "The story is that he was gathering some scrap lumber near the fence to take home and make some furniture for his family. The guard reportedly ordered him to stop, but he didn't and started to run away. So the guard shot him. People say the man was shot from the *front*, not the back."

Shaking his head, Yoneichi concluded, "Nobody knows exactly what happened and that's added more fuel to the fire. It's getting pretty crazy out there."

Papa-san added, "I heard that at Topaz [internment camp] apparently an old man was shot when he tried to prevent his puppy from escaping under the barbed-wire fence. The man couldn't have gone very far. Sounds like the sentries are getting trigger-happy. Things are getting out of hand."

Looking at each of us, he quietly advised, "Given the unstable environment, let's not draw any attention to ourselves."

Sitting on my cot not feeling anything, I said nothing, but wondered, *How much more bad news can I take? I feel the world shutting down around me.* We had always been a peace-loving family, but now we were hearing about threats, killings, and violent behavior all around us.

~⦿~

At last the deadline arrived for turning in our questionnaires. Papa-san wanted us to privately and deliberately discuss how each one of us planned to vote. This was unusual. In many families, people were expected to vote the way the father wanted.

Papa-san sat down on one cot and I sat down opposite him while Yoneichi went over and gently shut the door. Then he came and sat down beside me.

Mama-san said, "While we think about all of this, I'm going to fix us some tea."

I watched her reach for the jar filled with green tea leaves. She sprinkled a pinch or two into the pot and poured in hot water. Watching Mama-san do this simple ritual as she had done hundreds of times in the past helped to calm me. We were about to make our momentous decision.

This would be my first adult decision. My parents were treating me as an equal. The seriousness of the situation scared me, but we were all together.

After a few minutes, Mama-san poured the fragrant beverage into four cups and served each of us before she sat down beside Papa-san. They sat close together just as Yoneichi and I did. We quietly and thoughtfully sipped our tea.

Finally, we leaned toward each other, putting our heads close together to speak in hushed tones. We knew other people in the barracks could hear our conversations so we spoke quietly so no one overheard.

Papa-san started by saying, "We're all familiar with the growing tension in our camp. This questionnaire has created much discussion and disagreement within our community, but nevertheless each of us must decide how we will respond. So our choice is to vote 'Yes Yes' or 'No No.'"

I listened intently as Papa-san spoke. "In spite of everything, this is still a good country with all kinds of possibilities. This time will pass. It is important for me to maintain faith that this will all work out eventually for the best."

He paused and looked at each of us in turn. "I choose to vote 'Yes Yes.'"

I looked at Mama-san's face; it was calm like Papa-san's. She, like so many *Issei* mothers, had long ago established a **subordinate** but significant role within the family. But in this situation, it was clear to me that Mama-san had made her own decision based upon her values and hopes for the future. I did not expect her to defy or disagree with Papa-san, but I knew she would bring a different perspective.

"I know there are many troubling things going on here at Tule Lake and in many of the other camps," Mama-san began. "It's hard to understand what the government will do next, but no matter what, it is very important to us that we talk about these things so we understand and help each other. It is vitally important to Papa-san and to me that we all stay together in whatever we decide to do."

With a firm voice and a steady gaze at Yoneichi and me, she stated, "I, too, vote 'Yes Yes.'"

Most mothers would use a steady gaze to tell their children how they *must* vote, but that is not what I perceived. Her glance showed her confidence that Yoneichi and I would make the right choice for ourselves.

There was a long silence. Outside, the wind picked up, pushing dust into the cracks in the walls and the spaces between the barracks. Finally, Mama-san asked, "Yoneichi-san and Mary-san, how do you see it?"

I looked at Yoneichi, knowing how critical his decision would be. There was an important, unspoken cultural value that entered into this decision. It is called *oya-koko,* which means caring for one's parents beyond what is required. In our family, *oya-koko* was a definite part of our decision. Yoneichi and I felt as strongly about our parents as they did about us. We needed to make sure they would be cared for in their old age.

Yoneichi sat erect, held his head up, and spoke without hesitation. I noticed the same steady gaze that I saw in my parents' eyes. He looked at each of us. "My 'Yes-Yes' decision will mean that I must go into the Army and fight in the war. I'm prepared to do that. That is the one thing I can do to *prove* our family's loyalty to the United States."

Traditionally, Japanese men went into war expecting to die. This was a part of Japanese culture that persisted among the American-born Japanese. Yoneichi was willing to fight and die, if necessary.

When Yoneichi said, "Yes Yes," tears clouded my vision. He was going to war, and he could be killed fighting. My brother was my mentor, my trailblazer, who gave me his advice about my behavior or appearance—which I didn't always appreciate. I had followed in his footsteps.

Now, I had to make a decision. I felt trapped. Of course, I should be an obedient daughter and just follow my family's lead. But in my heart, I wanted to go in opposition to them because what happened wasn't right.

Everyone's eyes turned to me. My shoulders hunched up as I leaned forward gripping my teacup in both hands. I agonized silently. *If I agree to vote "Yes Yes," I will be agreeing with the rest of the family that Yoneichi will have to go to war. If I vote "No No," I could be separated from my family.*

As my family awaited my decision, still I hesitated. Although I knew "Yes Yes" was the right choice, it broke my heart. It felt like I was giving in to the bully in the schoolyard.

I took a deep breath and at last, a calmness settled over me. The tension in my chest relaxed. Instead of loyalty to any illusion of country, my commitment was to the reality of the love within my own family. *They* were my country. Each one looked at me with kind eyes and with a slight bow of their heads. Each one acknowledged my place as a full member of this family.

Leaning my head near my brother and parents, I looked at each of them and said, "Yes Yes."

⊰◉⊱

It took me more than fifty years to understand and appreciate the sacrifices of those who chose "No No." The "No-No people" fought for our rights in a very different way that many traditional Japanese families did not understand during World War II.

Even when the U.S. government threatened the "No-No people" with violation of the Espionage Act, punishable by a $10,000 fine and up to twenty years imprisonment, the "No-No people" stood their ground. We were in agreement that our people's civil rights had been violated and the order for the evacuation was unjust. The Loyalty Oath was intended to separate the loyals from the disloyals, but it ended up separating Japanese Americans for reasons that had nothing to do with loyalty.

Knowing what I know now as a woman in her 80s who has lived a long life, I see that I judged the "No-No people" wrongly. Now, I weep for the people whom the U.S. government labeled as disloyal and punished harshly. The "No-No people" were denied leave clearance from the internment camps and they were denied other privileges. Some were tried as criminals, convicted on flimsy evidence and jailed. Through all of this, most of them did not receive fair legal counsel.

Most troubling of all to me is the way we Japanese Americans condemned our own people because the "No Nos" chose a different way in which to respond. Although it was not obvious to me at the time, the "No-No people" were also victims of intimidation perpetuated by those who voted "Yes Yes."

For decades after the war, many people in the Japanese-American community shunned and excluded the "No Nos." Now, I understand that it took tremendous courage for those who voted "No No" to face rejection by American society and by their own people.

My hope is that the position of the "No Nos" will be understood and accepted as worthy of the highest form of respect. Dissent is an essential expression of democracy.

Heart Mountain Internment Camp in Wyoming was the third camp Mary and her family moved to.

MARY MATSUDA GRUENEWALD COLLECTION

CHAPTER EIGHTEEN

HEART MOUNTAIN INTERNMENT CAMP

I was greatly relieved by our family's decision.

The morning after our family meeting, Papa-san turned in our completed questionnaires. While I was worried about the consequences of our choices, that evening Yoneichi reminded us, "We'll have to keep our decision to ourselves. We don't want the 'No-No' guys to get wind of it."

The threats and beatings continued. One night I bolted upright in bed to the sound of many feet pounding on the ground outside our barrack. My family heard it, too. After the footsteps died in the distance and all was quiet again, I flopped back on my cot. It took awhile before I could drop back to sleep.

The following day we heard there had been a serious fight in the central part of our camp during the night. The camp administration called in the Army and imposed martial law. The soldiers immediately went from block to block, barrack to barrack, primarily in the central part of camp searching for the men who caused the violence. When the suspects were found and caught, they were locked up in the **stockade**—inside an already barbed-wire camp.

The soldiers with their rifles patrolled the camp daily, but the increasing tension and occasional uprisings made me more fearful. It was now eleven months since we had been evacuated from our home.

As the days passed, I became increasingly preoccupied with the question, *What will happen to us if the war doesn't go well for the United States?* And I couldn't help but consider, *This uprising might be the excuse the Army needs to kill us all.*

A couple of months after signing the Loyalty Oath, Yoneichi and a friend decided it was time to register for the draft. This required a hazardous journey past the central part of the internment camp and into the administration building. The two friends decided Yoneichi would go in first, and if he saw any sign of danger, he would give a hand signal, and his friend would run away immediately.

It was frightening for me to hear them making their plans. When they left, I waited nervously for them to return. About an hour later they got back. Yoneichi seemed casual about the whole thing. "It was easy," he said. "I'm glad I got that out of the way."

◦◉◦

The *Tulean Dispatch* published an official announcement from the government of the process for segregating the internees according to the way we voted. All internment camps would be affected. The program was scheduled to begin around September 1.

The Director of the WRA felt that the longer the two divergent groups lived in such close proximity, the greater the chances for rioting and bloodshed. The WRA had plans to divide the internees into four groups with different degrees of loyalty, ranging from "loyal to the United States" to "loyal to Japan."

Unfortunately, the real-life complexities of the internees did not fit so neatly into these four categories. Although the registration process had been fraught with confusion, the segregation program had been carefully planned. The WRA learned from the disaster it created with the original questionnaire. This time, the administration gave the evacuees the opportunity to clearly identify if they were loyal or sympathetic to Japan or to the United States.

Based on their loyalties, this would determine which internment camp the WRA would send them to. If the government labeled internees as "disloyals," they stayed at Tule Lake for the duration of the war. The WRA granted the "loyals" clearance and assistance to move to one of the other nine camps, if desired. At that point, they could obtain clearance to leave the camps permanently.

Mary's graduation photo.

On July 16, 1943, I graduated with 397 seniors from Tri-State High School. My classmates and I dressed in caps and gowns and sat on benches lined up in front of the outdoor stage.

If we had been living at home, we would have been looking forward to all kinds of exciting future possibilities: going off to college, getting jobs, working independently, getting married, or traveling to foreign countries, just to mention a few. Despite the oppressive situation, we chose our class theme: "Today We Follow...Tomorrow We Lead."

At the graduation ceremony, a group of students who called themselves the Harmonaires sang "Invictus," a short poem written in 1875 by the English poet, William Henley. The composer, Bruno Huhn, put the poem to music.

INVICTUS

Out of the night that covers me,
Black as the pit from pole to pole,
I thank whatever gods may be
For my unconquerable soul....
I am the master of my fate
I am the captain of my soul.

The words of the song did not match my feelings at all. I was unclear about my identity and could not imagine being the master of my fate or the captain of my soul. All during my grade school and high school years at Vashon, I had been looking forward to high school graduation, believing my life would open. But now, the freedoms of that world had disappeared.

World events and national policies had swept away all the choices I had taken for granted. A few of my classmates did leave camp to continue their education, but for most of us, there was nothing to look forward to. It was more of the same monotonous routine.

By August 1943, the WRA completed most of the segregation decision-making. Based on our "Yes-Yes" vote, our family received orders and clearance to leave Tule Lake on September 13, 1943. We were sent to Heart Mountain Internment Camp in northwestern Wyoming. I was glad we were leaving this frightening place, but this move was harder than the last.

Over the past fourteen months I had developed close friendships with a number of people in our ward and in high school. Now, we would be separated again.

~ ◎ ~

As I rode the train with my family from Tule Lake to Heart Mountain, I was hopeful that this camp would be much better. Three days later we arrived at another treeless camp with the familiar barracks covered in black tar paper and surrounded by barbed-wire fences. My heart sank. I didn't know there could be so many bleak and barren places in this country. Looking to the sagebrush-dotted hills beyond, I could see a rock formation shaped like a heart, which was the reason for the name of the camp.

I wondered, *Could it be possible to hope that this camp might be safer and people would have more heart here?* It would be in this desolate place that we would face one of our hardest times as a family.

A truck took us to our new residence at block 12, barrack 8, and apartment C. The truck driver pointed to an outer doorway with a recessed alcove behind it that led to apartments C and D. "You'll be in apartment C on the left," the truck driver said.

"Oh, there is one entryway to two apartments?" Yoneichi asked.

"Yes. Last winter it was so cold here, down in the 20s most of the time," explained the truck driver. "These alcoves keep out much of the wind, dust, and cold whenever people go in and out of their apartments. You'll be glad it's made that way."

I was curious about the people with whom we would be sharing the alcove. After we put our luggage inside, Papa-san and Yoneichi once again went looking for straw and ticking for mattresses. Since our room was the same size as the one we just left in Tule Lake, it didn't take much imagination for Mama-san and me to set it up. Then we went outdoors and looked around.

The environment here was not unlike the one at Tule Lake. All the barracks looked exactly alike. We went next door to apartment D. Mama-san bowed to the older couple, introduced us, and greeted them. The gentleman bowed and returned our greeting. "Hello, we are the Yamaguchis. Welcome." His wife looked at us and nodded her head. She appeared frail and withdrawn. They were a quiet couple; there would never be any cause for concern from that side of the building.

We went to the room on the other side of ours, to apartment B, and responded to the invitation, "Come in." There were four young people lounging on their cots. When we introduced ourselves, the older girl sat up and said, "I'm Tomoko Ogata, and these are my brothers, Juro and Ken, and my sister Mariko. Dad is over at the post office right now. I'll tell him you moved in next door."

Tomoko and her brothers were attractive young people, possibly in their twenties. I guessed Mariko to be around thirteen. I learned their mother had died. It didn't take long for us to discover that the Ogatas were very sociable. Young people were continually going in and out of their apartment most of the day and late into the evening.

Like the barracks in Pinedale Assembly Center and Tule Lake, the triangular shaped opening between the walls and the roof allowed noise to echo throughout the barracks. To our dismay, the loud music, talking, laughing, and arguments next door at the Ogatas became a frequent source of disturbance.

Once again we were in the midst of other families in another big prison camp. Guards in the watchtowers had become such a common part of our daily lives that they could be ignored. Yet, I was aware they could shoot if we made any move they interpreted as out of line.

I had come to this new camp hopeful things would be much better, that I could go about my life feeling safer and freer. My original optimism quickly faded away into a boring routine.

All of my friends from Tule Lake were gone, and I had to make an effort to make new friends. I had already graduated from high school so it was more difficult to make friends. The only thing familiar was my family and the endless days with nothing to do.

~◉~

A national crisis had occurred following the imprisonment of Japanese Americans in 1942. The labor force was strained. Many men were serving in the military, and civilians, many of them women, worked in munitions factories, shipyards or other war industries. This resulted in thousands of acres of deteriorating crops due to the lack of a labor force.

Japanese-American farmers on the West Coast had produced much of the fruit and vegetables for the western United States. Now, they were no longer available to provide the necessary food supplies. Although Japanese Americans were initially seen as threats to American security and removed from our farms, now the government decided we were essential. Japanese-American labor was needed to save the nation's crops.

When Japanese Americans were rounded up and put in internment camps, the U.S government asked the state governors from Utah, Arizona, Nevada, Montana, Idaho, New Mexico, Wyoming, Washington, and Oregon to allow Japanese Americans to voluntarily relocate to their states. Most of the governors were strongly opposed to this idea. They didn't want any Japanese in their states—even in internment camps.

Now, a little more than a year later, these same governors suddenly saw the benefit of having the Japanese Americans come to their states to save their crops. Responding to this gigantic need, the WRA made temporary or seasonal leaves available to people in the camps and urged them to apply for clearance in eastern Oregon, Washington, Idaho, Utah, Montana, and Wyoming. This meant Japanese Americans could leave the camps temporarily if they received clearance from the FBI. This seasonal leave appealed especially to the restless young *Nisei* men.

We had been reading about this latest development in the camp's newspaper, the *Heart Mountain Sentinel*. One evening, my brother brought up the idea of getting a seasonal leave to work on a farm.

"I think it's a good idea," Papa-san replied. "You'll have a chance to get out of camp for a few months. I read that the farmers who need laborers to come and save their crops assure your transportation, housing, and safety. I think it's okay to go."

My mother and I agreed. It was all right for Yoneichi to go, but I was not ready to leave. I had never been on my own before. I had not given any thought to living alone nor how I would make my own way in the world.

The war in the Pacific was still raging, and I was still coping with feelings of self-doubt and shame. My greatest fear was facing more anti-Japanese prejudice. The evacuation process had devastated me, and I was too fearful of leaving my family.

Yoneichi became one of the 10,000 people who left the internment camps on temporary leave to harvest crops in the fall of 1943. This was the first time we were separated as a family. Yoneichi worked for about two months harvesting sugar beets in Idaho and Washington. We were so glad when he returned. Yoneichi seemed more self-assured as he shared his stories. They were a mixture of positive experiences and difficult encounters when he went into nearby towns for various services.

"We were treated well by some of the farmers when we first got there," he reported, "but when we got through harvesting the crops, we were no longer welcomed. One time a couple of us decided to get haircuts. We noticed a sign outside one barbershop, 'No Japs Allowed.' We moved on until we found a better place and we got good haircuts there.

"In one place in Idaho, we were having trouble getting groceries because they wouldn't sell to us," Yoneichi continued. "So we had to leave the store empty handed. I was amazed when a white man brought a variety of groceries to us in his van, and we could buy from him."

Papa-san remarked, "He was a courageous man for doing that."

"We told him how much we appreciated what he did and that we were concerned because he could be labeled 'Jap lover.' But he didn't seem to be too worried about that."

I listened to one of Yoneichi's friends tell a similar story about his experiences topping sugar beets and gathering potatoes. "I went to help out with the harvest and made pretty good money doing it," the friend explained. "Our boss was glad to have us come and help with the harvest. But when it was over, we were Japs again. He didn't want us around. I didn't like it that we were welcomed only when we were needed."

At the time, we did not know of significant changes going on in the outside world regarding our future and the treatment of Japanese Americans. A major debate took place in the nation's capital between the War Department and General John L. DeWitt, the commander of the Western Defense Command who pushed for and carried out the evacuation of Japanese Americans on the West Coast. Now, The War Department no longer believed that loyal Japanese Americans should be excluded from the West Coast. Sadly, the military was unwilling to reverse its orders and General DeWitt was allowed to keep Japanese Americans imprisoned in the camps.

During the first half of 1943, propaganda and hateful feelings against the Japanese Americans flared up. Various organizations, citizens' groups, and politicians began lobbying to **banish** Japanese Americans permanently from the United States. Major newspapers such as the *San Francisco Examiner* and the *Los Angeles Times* joined in the escalating attack on Japanese Americans. They wanted the Japanese Americans to be sent "back to Japan"—forever.

However, by mid-July 1943, the hateful tide of racism was beginning to turn. In time, the propaganda of half-truths and lies about Japanese Americans was replaced by a more humane and rational approach to the whole internment question. As a result, General DeWitt was labeled a "military **zealot**." The military relieved him of his duties with the Western Defense Command in the fall of 1943.

By year's end, key people in the government urged the return of the internees to their homes. What probably helped ease anti-Japanese sentiment in the United States was the fact that America and its allies began to win the war in the South Pacific in the summer of 1943.

Some Japanese Americans turned to the legal system to fight being imprisoned in internment camps. They sued the U.S. government for illegally forcing them into camps and depriving them of their rights as U.S. citizens. At the time, I was unaware of the Japanese Americans who fought legal battles for justice. The slow-moving legal system took a long time to resolve these court cases and the Japanese Americans did not get the justice they sought.

One well-known case, *Korematsu v. United States,* involved a Japanese American from the San Francisco area, Fred Toyosaburo Korematsu, who refused to evacuate. He was in love with a Caucasian woman and did not want to leave. The U.S. government arrested him and convicted Korematsu of remaining in a military zone at a time when Japanese were excluded from living on the West Coast.

In December 1944, the Supreme Court ruled that Korematsu was wrong and the U.S. government had the right to force him to an internment camp. Years later, this decision would be described as one of the most forbidding and unreasonable opinions in the history of the Supreme Court, silencing a citizen's right to justice under the law. Basically, the Supreme Court decided racial discrimination was constitutional in cases of "national emergency."

This judicial decision still stands some sixty-five years later and the U.S. government could still legally imprison groups of people if it declared an emergency.

CHAPTER NINETEEN

REMEMBERING
TWENTY YEARS FROM NOW

Our hopes of returning home seemed more remote than ever.

The war was fierce with battles in full force in Europe and the South Pacific. Everything outside of the barbed-wire fence was beyond my reach. Reclaiming our freedom and regaining our status as loyal citizens seemed a long way off.

My sense of isolation and impending doom intensified. I kept thinking about the time when the Army would call on Yoneichi to fight in the war.

I also worried about our farm. One day I overheard Papa-san say to Mama-san, "We haven't heard anything from Mack. I wonder how the strawberry harvest went this summer. I hope it went all right." We had entrusted the care of our farm to Mack when we were forced to evacuate. "Yes, we haven't heard, but if anyone could manage our farm it would be Mack," Mama-san replied. "Let's just wait and see."

I had never concerned myself with the business dealings of the farm; that was Papa-san and Yoneichi's responsibility. But suddenly I realized that something was not right. Before we left Vashon Island, Yoneichi had a lawyer draw up a contract regarding the operation of the farm in our absence. In that document the deputy sheriff on Vashon and Yoneichi had agreed that all profits and expenses for our farm would be divided 50/50. That evening, I was stunned to overhear Yoneichi and Papa-san discuss that some other farmers had heard updates on the status of their farms on Vashon, but we hadn't, despite letters of inquiry.

I began to worry. *Was he stealing our money? Was he paying our bills? Could we lose our home so there would be nothing to go home to?* A nagging suspicion was growing that something was wrong, but there was nothing we could do about it.

◦◎◦

The day finally came when Yoneichi received a letter from the draft board. Papa-san looked very grave as he handed the envelope to his son. Yoneichi paused for a moment before opening the envelope, then he read it in silence. There was another long pause after Yoneichi finished, then he looked up at the three of us.

"I have been very fortunate," he said. "I had a good draft number, but now the time has come. I have three months to get ready. I leave for basic training at the end of June."

I couldn't deny the inevitable any longer. I ran from the apartment with tears streaming down my face, oblivious to the stares of others. I collapsed into a pile behind our barrack and sobbed, brokenhearted. Soon, I felt Mama-san's arms around me. I reached over to hold her, my face against hers, our tears mingled together. Many long minutes passed before either of us could talk.

"I don't want him to go!" I finally gasped. "I don't want him to go!"

"Yes, I know," Mama-san whispered quietly into my ear. "I don't want him to go, either, but he must."

We spent a long time holding each other and talking.

A few days later, Mama-san told me about an ancient Japanese tradition, a stitched **talisman** for Yoneichi to wear into battle. It was called a *senninbari*, a thousand-stitch belt.

Mama-san bought a yard of white cotton fabric, black embroidery thread, sewing needles of various sizes, a ruler, and an embroidery hoop. Back in our room, I sat near her as she took the ruler and marked out a rectangle in the middle of the fabric. Along each side she marked off dots, approximately three millimeters apart, and filled in the rest of the spaces between until there were a thousand dots in tight, neat little rows.

The embroidery hoop held the fabric tight and made it much easier to handle. Cutting off approximately twelve inches of the embroidery thread, she threaded one end through the needle and made a knot in the other.

As Mama-san worked, she explained, "It is very important that Yoneichi-san have this *senninbari* to carry with him while he is away from us at war. This will give him courage and strength when he has this symbol of our love.

"According to tradition, this *senninbari* carries the care and support of the one thousand women and girls who will make their stitches for him. Only stitches made by people praying for his safe return have the power to protect him from the bullets of the enemy."

As Mama-san was about to make the first knot in the fabric, she took a deep breath, bowed her head, and closed her eyes. She remained still for a long minute, her face composed, as her lips moved silently in prayer. She raised her head, then made the knot.

Then, she turned, bowed slightly and handed me the *senninbari* to make the next stitch.

I bowed my head as tears welled up. *My only brother is going off to fight in the war to prove our family's loyalty,* I thought. *He is my trailblazer.*

When Yoneichi was a senior and I was a sophomore, I remember feeling so proud of him when he was elected secretary of the student body. A school advisor later told me how much she admired his many abilities in scholarship, athletics, and friendly relationships with all the students in school.

Although he was short, Yoneichi was fast and fearless, and made the Vashon High School varsity football team. To help him improve his skills, I learned to pass spirals so he could practice catching the football on the run.

What if he never returns from the war? I wondered. Crying, I couldn't see where the next dot was in the fabric. Mama-san put her hand on my arm and waited as I regained my composure.

"Yoneichi-san will appreciate having this made by you and me and all the others. This is the time for faith that it will help to keep him safe."

I completed my stitch.

Mama-san and I then began to make the rounds of our neighbors and friends, asking each woman and girl to make her mark on the *senninbari*. Mama-san kept adding lengths to the thread to insure that it was continuous. In a way, Mama-san was the continuous thread that had kept the tapestry of our family intact throughout these years.

We moved from barrack to barrack until we had covered the entire ward. Beyond that, we relied on the recommendations of our Vashon friends to help us find those who would be willing to contribute a stitch for Yoneichi.

Most of the women we asked understood our position and made their stitches enthusiastically. But one woman smugly said to Mama-san, "I don't agree that the *Niseis* should fight for America but I'll make this stitch just for him. I still think you folks are foolish for letting him go."

Mama-san merely nodded her head in acknowledgment and expressed appreciation for her making her knot, but I was outraged! I hated her! How could she be so rude?

Within days we had one thousand stitches.

A few evenings later in our room, Mama-san bowed slightly in front of Yoneichi and said, "Yoneichi-san, here is a *senninbari* that the ladies and girls in our neighborhood made for you to take with you into battle. For hundreds of years men have carried this symbol of protection before they left their loved ones. This belt has special powers to protect you from the enemy. Remember, there were one thousand of us who made this for you. All of us will pray to God for your safe return."

Yoneichi received it with both hands, closed his eyes, and bowed his head as he raised the gift to his forehead. After a moment, Yoneichi raised his head, and with tenderness in his eyes said, "*Arigato gozaimasu* (thank you) Mama-san. I will keep it every day with the New Testament in my breast pocket, over my heart."

We bought a picture of a tiger for Yoneichi and hung it on the wall opposite the entryway, a place to catch our eye whenever we came into our apartment. The tiger is a symbol of strength and protection, and we wanted that for Yoneichi.

~◎~

One evening when the four of us returned from dinner, I was feeling especially gloomy. I sat lost in memories of our evenings on Vashon. Then my sweet memories slipped into my despair and this strange world—the internment camps—I had been thrown into.

The voice in my head started in: *I've been caught in the reach of the sweeping searchlight; caught with yellow skin, slant eyes, black straight hair with buckteeth. I am like the "yellow-bellied" soldiers on the front page of* Time *magazine, clutching helpless women and children as they trample the burning cities of America!*

I could not shake the feeling that I was bad and not to be trusted. That was why I was in prison here, and there was nothing I could do about any of this.

All the things they had used to divert my attention in the camps hadn't changed a thing for me. *They can have their sports, their eve-*

ning *variety shows, the movies, and the dances!* I thought. *They can have it all! I'm still in prison and isolated!*

Then I worried about our farm and the deputy sheriff on Vashon. *We haven't heard from him. Is he stealing our money? We can't trust him. He's going to take our home and farm away from us!*

Quickly my worries jumped to Yoneichi. *He is going into the Army and will be sent off to war in Europe to be killed and when he's gone, they'll come after the rest of us. And no one can save me!*

Within minutes I was emotionally sunk.

I looked over at Yoneichi who had his back to me. In a few weeks, I might never see him again. A churning feeling rose in my gut and spilled over, out of control.

I bobbed my head and slapped my thighs with my hands as I burst out, "I can't stand it any more! Yoneichi is going to die! We're going to lose our home and farm forever! Why? We haven't done anything wrong! We're still prisoners! God has abandoned us! There's nothing that can save us! Not even you, Mama-san!" I sobbed.

The sound of people walking by our barrack was in the background. No one moved or uttered a sound in our apartment. My family sat stunned for a long time, all of us looking down at the floor. I was as horrified as the others, unable to take back what a moment before I had been unable to contain.

In the shocked silence, a look of calm determination came over Mama-san. She recognized the anguish in my words and realized that I was—that we were—at a crossroads. The truth had been told, and there was no turning back.

She looked up and quietly said, "You are not alone in your feelings, Mary-san, because I have them too."

I let out a sobbing breath, astonished. "You do?"

As I looked at her through my tears, her face came into focus. It was warm, sad, and old.

Why had I never seen her despair? I wondered. I knew the sad stories of her parents' deaths.

Mama-san sat on her cot across from me, the stress of so much loss clouding her eyes. She reached across and took my hands in both of her warm ones. She held my hands for a moment, then got up and sat down beside me. Placing her face against mine and wiping my tears with her handkerchief, she put her arms around my shoulders and rocked me gently back and forth, back and forth. Papa-san and Yoneichi gathered around us in silent support as my sobbing quieted.

Then she said softly and slowly, "There are times when things happen to us that we can't explain. We have no control. We are here because of forces outside of our family. We had no part in creating any of this, but we cannot expect to live in a world in which there is no pain or fear, where everything goes along without disturbing events. Our situation could be unbearable, unless..." and after a long pause and a faraway, serene look on her face, she added quietly, "unless we reconsider how we will face it."

At first I didn't understand. I relaxed a little, but still I felt we were trapped.

"Let's imagine," she said after a thoughtful silence, "that we are now twenty years into the future, looking back on our situation as it is right now."

Mama-san looked at Yoneichi, then glanced briefly at Papa-san. "Some of us *may* survive this time. Twenty years from now, we may have nothing more than the memories of how we conducted ourselves with dignity and courage during this difficult time."

She paused. "What kind of memories do we want to have *then* of how we faced these difficulties *now?*"

Mama-san looked at me and nodded. Her tender smile deepened the dimples in her cheeks and the laughing lines at her eyes. She dropped her arms from my shoulders and took my hands again.

I felt disoriented, dazed. Suddenly, reality didn't matter. It was as if I was released from my body, from camp, from suffering. I felt like I was floating in space with no boundaries to control me—just a profound feeling of freedom.

What kind of memories do we want to have then of how we faced these difficulties now? I asked myself.

What a startling suggestion! It felt like the pressure of a massive balloon in my chest suddenly deflated. I could breathe. Mama-san had taken this wretched situation and transformed it into one filled with hope and possibility. My heart opened up to what I had just heard. The darkness of my depression began to lift and for the first time I knew in my core I could choose freedom and a different attitude.

They can trap my body, I told myself, *but not my spirit and not my future.*

Papa-san and Yoneichi's bodies and facial expressions relaxed, too. Their breathing was deeper and slower just like mine. The tension in our shoulders eased.

Yoneichi was the first to speak. "I'd like to remember that we agreed as a family to do whatever it took to prove our loyalty to our homeland, America. I want us all to be proud of our family." We all nodded thoughtfully.

Papa-san looked around at each of us and spoke with obvious pride. "I'd like to remember that we listened to each other, but decided things as a family and acted as one, with courage and honor."

Then Mama-san said, "I'd like to remember that during this time we never lost our love for each other and developed hope and faith that we would come out of this time stronger and with a greater appreciation for each other." Each of us smiled in agreement.

Outside, the sky had grown darker with the approach of night, leaving our four faces illuminated by the single light bulb suspended over our heads. What was so clear to me was the power of Mama-san's love and faith and hope in me and in our family.

Just as her arms surrounded me, I felt enveloped in her love. I was no longer alone, even in my despair. Our family could continue to face together whatever was ahead.

Listening to everyone else, I realized it was time for me to lay aside my bitterness, self-pity, and feelings of inferiority. I blushed with embarrassment, but everyone nodded at me, waiting.

Taking a deep breath I said in a shaky voice, "I'd like to look back and remember that, in the middle of this crisis, I was able to see my family take everything that was happening and use it all to help me grow up." In that moment, with their patience and love, I became an adult.

⊰◎⊱

That evening, as had been our custom, we had our snack before bed. On Vashon our snack might have been a piece of watermelon, cantaloupe, persimmon, or pear. Or it could have been a slice of delicious peach pie with a flaky crust or chocolate cake with white, creamy frosting. But here at camp, we each had a soda cracker. That was all we had for a bedtime snack.

Mama-san suggested we imagine what kind of treat we were having that evening. The others kept changing their imaginary dessert selection, but mine was always the same—the most luscious banana split ever created.

That night as Mama-san gave me a soda cracker to eat I received it in my open palms, bowed my head, and closed my eyes. I placed the cracker into my mouth, and the dry saltiness slowly dissolved, just as it had every evening since our arrival at Heart Mountain.

But this time, the sweet richness of the ice cream positively exploded in my mouth, the strawberry seeds crunching delicately between my teeth, the thick caramel slowly enveloping my tongue. The banana was a perfect state of ripeness and the chocolate thick and smooth. Even the nuts and cherry combined for a sweet crunch. I swallowed, raised my head, opened my eyes, and smiled with the sweetness.

~ CHAPTER TWENTY ~

YONEICHI GOES TO WAR

Days flew by.

Yoneichi's dreaded departure was rapidly approaching. As more young men left the internment camp for the military, I could feel the tension in the air.

One evening as we gathered for our evening snack, Yoneichi started to act silly like he used to do back home. Sitting at his usual place on his cot, he said, "Look at this."

He pulled his lower eyelids down with the thumb and middle fingers of one hand revealing the whites of his eyes. Taking the index finger of the other hand and pushing his nose upwards, his face looked all squished together. When he rolled his eyes around in circles, he looked so ridiculous we couldn't keep from laughing. His comic behavior broke the tension. It felt wonderful to focus on something funny. Then Yoneichi made another funny face and we laughed so hard we had to hold our stomachs.

Mama-san was not to be outdone.

She said, "Here's Mrs. Watanabe and Mrs. Yamamoto trying to be polite and urging the other to take the first cup of tea."

First she'd bow as one woman and then quickly turn to bow as the other, like two mechanical dolls with incessant bobbing heads. As Mrs. Watanabe, Mama-san repeatedly bowed as she said with an exaggerated voice accent, "*Purreesu, Yamamoto-san,*

habu somu cukisu. (Please, Yamamoto-san, have some cookies.)
They are inferior to your wonderful delicacies, but I ask you to
do me the honor of having some."

I clapped my hands and laughingly said, "I can just hear her
saying that."

Then she turned her body around to portray Mrs. Yamamoto
in a high-pitched voice with a different regional dialect, all the
while repeatedly bobbing her entire upper body in an exaggerated deep bow.

We laughed until tears rolled down our cheeks. Even Papa-
san, who was usually quiet and dignified, opened his mouth and
laughed out loud. When she stopped, she looked at us with a
mischievous innocent look on her face, obviously pleased with her
successful imitation. That got us laughing even more.

⤙◉⤚

The June days got longer and hotter. Every few days the wind
would abruptly kick up sand and dust, sending us running for
cover. Yoneichi would be leaving soon for the Army. There was no
way for us to take cover or overlook this fact.

Finally, that morning arrived. We all ate breakfast in the mess
hall and sat closer together than usual. The scrambled eggs didn't
taste good, the toast was cold and dry, and the coffee was bitter. I
wasn't hungry.

When we got back to our room, Yoneichi slowly looked around
the apartment. It was as though he was trying to imprint the setting in his memory. We sat down on two cots and faced each other
as we had each evening before each family discussion time.

Mama-san quietly made a final pot of tea. We were silent with
our individual thoughts as we sipped our fragrant tea. Papa-san
held his cup in his left palm as he slowly turned it round and
round with his right hand. His hand trembled a bit as he brought
it up to his lips to take a sip.

Finally, Mama-san began to speak softly. "We have a wonderful family. Yoneichi-san and Mary-san, I am so proud of both of you. And now, Yoneichi-san, it has come time for you to leave us. Let us remember the good times we have shared. That will help us all as you leave us."

Yoneichi looked tenderly at her and replied, "I will. Yes, ours is a wonderful family. It will help me to think about all of us together."

Papa-san looked at Yoneichi and with a steady, strong voice said, *"Shikkari shite kudasai, neh?"* (Be strong for all of us, all right?) Then he continued in Japanese, "There may be many difficult times ahead for you but whatever hardships come, be strong and bring honor to our family."

"I will, Papa-san," Yoneichi replied firmly as he nodded his head.

Mama-san added, "You will be in our thoughts every day. Would you like us to pray together now?"

"Yes, Mama-san. That will help me."

Mama-san looked upward as she spoke clearly and slowly, *"Kami sama,* (God), this is a very difficult time for all of us." After a moment she continued. "We know Yoneichi-san carries the burden for our family and for all other Japanese families to fight with courage and bring honor to our community. Guide and protect him. May his battles be fought with a pure heart. We know You will be with him wherever he goes. Thank You for your constant presence with him and with each of us, giving us strength and hope and love. In the name of *Kami sama,* Amen."

She bowed her head and closed her eyes. All of us were silent. When we raised our heads, Mama-san looked at Yoneichi with such tenderness in her eyes.

He said, "Mama-san, thank you. I will carry that prayer and the *senninbari* with me wherever I go."

Then he turned to me and said gently, "This will be a difficult time for our folks. Take good care of them for me, okay? Doing that will help me the most."

Japanese American soldiers prepare to leave camp for war. Minidoka, 1944.

WING LUKE MUSEUM

"I promise," I whispered, trying to control the tremor in my voice.

Yoneichi looked at each of us and with a steady voice added, "We've had a good life together on the farm, and I'm grateful for this time of remembering all the good things that have been a part of our family. That will help me a lot while I have to be away."

Yoneichi stood up and gazed at each of us. "I'm proud to be going on behalf of all of us. You know my good friend, Sinch, will be going at the same time. We're both going to Fort Blanding in Florida, so we may be together quite a bit of the time. Try not to worry. I'll be careful."

Then he picked up his bag, and we accompanied him silently to the front gate where a bus waited for the men who were leaving. Like us, members of other families were there to see their sons leave. Everyone was quiet. It was hard to engage in small talk while we waited. Never had I felt so close to my brother, and I braced myself against the time of parting. We had all dreaded this moment.

My brother turned to me and I wrapped my arms around him. I didn't want to let go of him. All I could say was, "Be careful. I'll be praying for you every day."

As he looked into my eyes, he said, "Take good care of the folks. You know how important that is to me. It's up to you now, you know."

I nodded in acknowledgment. Just before he stepped into the bus he turned, lifted his hand in a motionless good-bye and said, "Thank you for everything. Take good care of each other and try not to worry."

He turned away and boarded the bus. We watched to see where he would sit, and we huddled close together in front of the window where we could see him. Other families were doing the same thing with their departing sons.

As the bus eased away, he returned our wave and smiled bravely. I watched the bus move towards the horizon. I could not control my tears. Even Papa-san's eyes were teary, but being the stoic head of our household he struggled to contain his emotions.

We stood a long while looking in the direction the bus had gone. We all knew without saying—this might be the last time we saw him.

Finally, I turned to Mama-san. "I hope he comes back to us alive."

And Mama-san whispered through her tears, "Let us pray he does."

When we returned to our apartment, I looked at his tidy, empty cot next to mine. All three of us sat looking at his cot, each of us deep in thought and prayer for our beloved Yoneichi.

᙭᙭

Yoneichi departed for basic training about two weeks after D-Day, which was the Allied Forces' invasion of Normandy, France on June 6, 1944. This was the largest land and naval invasion of all time. The Allies landed on the beaches of Normandy to fight Nazi Germany. This would become the first step to victory in Europe for the Allied Forces. Newspapers were filled with reports of terrible fighting, some wins, and heavy losses. I didn't want to keep imagining Yoneichi dead in Europe, but I couldn't help it.

I went through the activities of my day mechanically, almost in a trance. All I had now were memories. I thought back to the times when Yoneichi would stay up until 3 o'clock in the morning working on his calculus problems. Or the playful bantering we had about my love for classical music and his teasing questions of why I was listening to Beethoven and Bach.

I couldn't keep from crying. Repeatedly, I thought, *My only brother has gone off to fight a war for a country that is keeping us imprisoned like criminals.*

~⚙~

Years later, I would tell my grandson, Matthew, how his grand uncle, Yoneichi, was like the brave Momotaro in the classic Japanese fairy story, "Peach Boy." He went off to war to fight the giants that were causing great destruction in the world. Now, I understood how Momotaro's elderly parents must have felt as he left them to go fight for peace.

CHAPTER TWENTY-ONE

NURSING SCHOOL

Mama-san looked sad. In the days following Yoneichi's departure, she would brush away an occasional tear and heave a big sigh. The three of us sat closer together in the evening. We didn't talk much; we were with our thoughts and silent prayers for Yoneichi's safety and courage.

My parents looked forward to Yoneichi's letters, which were always written in Japanese. This pleased them. Occasionally, I would get a separate letter from Yoneichi written in English, but I received most of my information about his activities through his letters to our parents.

Days stretched into weeks, but each day and each week was the same as before—depressing and directionless. In one of those aimless, dreary days, I came to the realization that I was focusing only on what *wasn't* in my life. I asked myself, *Is this the way to live, always in the shadow of the past? What if some day I wake up and realize that I could have gone places but didn't? Will there be people I could have met and perhaps loved, but didn't?*

I was troubled by these thoughts. Now, I was nineteen years old—I'd better do something!

The next day I decided to go to the employment office in the camp's administration building. There was an opening as a nurse's aide in the camp hospital.

This reminded me of a conversation with Mama-san years earlier where she talked about the wonderful nurses who took care of her when she was in the hospital. This inspired me, so the following morning I submitted my application. An administrator quickly approved it and he asked me to report to the hospital the following morning. Apparently, they were very short of aides.

My first day on the job I received my nurse's aide uniform, a general orientation to the hospital, and an assignment on Wards 5 and 6, the medical and communicable disease wings. The head nurse gave me a thorough orientation on the care of these special patients.

I had to wear a nurse's facemask and an extra gown over my uniform to protect myself from germs. I also learned about a special hand washing technique to protect myself and not carry any **contaminants** to other patients. Then I was introduced to the hospital ward and given simple tasks such as passing out fresh water and reading materials to the patients.

Going to work each day and meeting people in the hospital gave me a whole new way of looking at my life. I was absorbed with learning how to take temperatures and blood pressures, how to give baths, make beds, and do various other nursing tasks. I enjoyed my interactions with the hospital staff and patients.

One day on the Communicable Disease Ward while I was taking fresh water around to the patients, I stopped and talked with a patient named John. He was a young man, perhaps 25 years old. He was thin, his skin almost transparent, and he had dark circles under his eyes. I asked him how he was doing.

He replied, "When you have **tuberculosis**, the main thing you have to do is rest. I read or listen to my radio, and talk with others on the ward. Other than that, there's really nothing else to do. It gets pretty boring." Then he looked at me standing next to his bed and added, "You get to go home after work and be with your

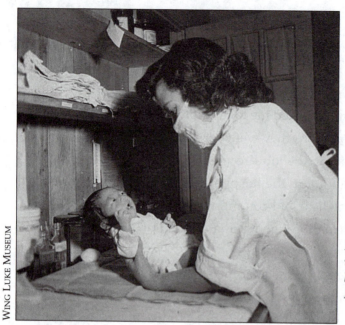

Hospital worker with new-born baby at Minidoka, 1943.

family, but I can't even do that. This is my family here," he said as he motioned to the other patients in the ward.

The young man had been in a **sanitarium** in Seattle for three years before the government transferred him to the internment camp. I wondered, *How could they think of this patient as a threat to the country's security?*

When I asked John how long he had to be in the hospital, he responded, "That's the heck of it. I don't have any idea when I'll be well enough to get out of bed. In a way, I have no future. I can't set any goals for my life."

As I went about my work that day my thoughts kept returning to John. His dismal predicament helped me appreciate what I did have. This job and the new people and experiences shifted my perspective and I began to find my life and work meaningful, despite the internment camp. My folks were pleased with my changes.

At the hospital, the Caucasian nursing supervisor, Miss Crosman, observed my interest and aptitude and suggested I become a registered nurse (R.N.). To encourage me, she gave me a pair of bandage scissors, which I later had engraved with the initials "M. M." for Mary Matsuda. Whenever I used them, I thought about Miss Crosman. Those scissors would stay with me in my purse throughout my fifty-year-career as an R.N.

As I continued to gain more experience, I often thought about Yoneichi and the *Nisei* men fighting overseas who needed medical attention. I thought about it for several days before I decided to talk with my parents. One evening while we were having our snack and tea, I said to my parents, "I wonder who is taking care of the *Niseis* injured in the war over in Europe."

I hesitated, then added, "I've been thinking that if I became a registered nurse, I'd like to go over to Europe to take care of them. What do you think about that?"

They both fell silent and looked thoughtful. Papa-san picked up his teacup, took a sip, then turned it round and round as he pondered this question.

Finally, Mama-san answered, "It would be very hard for us to have you go to war, too. But I know that if Yoneichi-san were wounded, I would want you there to do everything you could for him. I would be proud of you for doing that kind of work in that kind of setting for our boys."

Papa-san nodded in agreement and added, "You may be in a war zone. Things could be very primitive, and you would have to be resourceful, but you can do that. We would miss you, but it would be a comfort to us knowing you would be taking care of the wounded."

I was both relieved and pleased with their reaction. It would mean another sacrifice for them, but they were willing to let me go. Once again, their wisdom and love touched my heart.

~⊚~

Letters had been coming fairly regularly from my friend, Zola, in Hicksville, Ohio. One came about the time I had this discussion with my folks. I had written to Zola about my job as a nurse's aide in the hospital and how much I enjoyed the work. This time I included my thoughts about becoming a registered nurse and possibly going overseas to care for soldiers like my brother.

A reply came back immediately. Zola mentioned a new federal program that trained nurses for the war effort. She suggested talking to my nursing supervisor to find out if information was available in camp. If not, she would send it to me.

The next day the nursing supervisor took me to the bulletin board where information about the United States Cadet Nurse Corps was posted. I read over the information and sent off an application form.

A reply arrived promptly. I was delighted to learn the Corps would cover the cost of the training in a certified school of nursing anywhere in the country. There were openings at Jane Lamb Memorial Hospital in Clinton, Iowa. I sent in my application immediately.

A short time later, an acceptance letter arrived from the Director of Nursing at Jane Lamb Memorial Hospital. In her letter, the director noted that Jane Sasaki from Oregon has already been accepted in the current class. Her twin sister, Janet, and I would be in the next class beginning in September.

This was terrific news. I knew the Sasaki sisters because we were recent graduates from Tri State High School at the Tule Lake camp. Now, we would all be together in the same hospital. I could not have anticipated anything so wonderful.

As excited as I was about my own plans, I felt increasingly guilty about abandoning my parents. We needed to talk about their future.

"Mama-san, Papa-san, now that I am going to Iowa, I want to know what you want to do. Do you want to stay here?"

The two of them exchanged knowing glances. "Papa-san and I have been discussing this," Mama-san said. "It will be lonely here without both of you. We heard from the Umanis just last week. They have left camp to be with their son who is living on a farm in Nampa, Idaho. They have urged us to move to Minidoka Internment Camp, which is not too far away. Personally, I would like to be closer to the Umanis."

The Umanis could live outside of an internment camp because they had a son who had a successful farm outside of the evacuation zone. The majority of Japanese Americans had no such resources available. With Yoneichi now in the service, living outside of camp was not a practical option for my parents, but they could move to a camp closer to their dear friends. The Umanis had been their closest friends since their earliest years in the United States.

We had been at Heart Mountain for nearly a year, but we certainly didn't have any attachment to the place. I submitted an application to transfer all three of us to the Minidoka camp near Twin Falls, Idaho. Clearance arrived without much delay.

⠒◎⠒

It was time to move to our fourth internment camp, Minidoka, only this time it was by choice. My parents and I packed our few belongings and walked to the main gate of the camp. It was exciting to hand over our pass that permitted us to walk right through the gate without anyone stopping us. We boarded a Greyhound bus at the administration area of Heart Mountain and headed for the Minidoka Relocation Center near Twin Falls, Idaho.

The bus was crowded with servicemen and all kinds of folks traveling during wartime, using the bus instead of driving their cars due to **gas rationing**. During that twelve-hour trip, interrupted only by brief rest stops, the three of us had to stand along with several others in the crowded bus. We gripped the straps that hung from the ceiling or the seat backs as the bus negotiated turns and bumps in the road. Mama-san, now 52, and Papa-san, 67, looked as tired as I felt, but no one offered them a seat. None of us complained.

Finally, the bus stopped at Pocatello, Idaho for a layover before the last leg of the trip. We had a little time to see the town, so everyone went for a walk, eager to stretch their legs. We walked along the main street lined with stores, restaurants, and apartments.

All of the other passengers had drifted ahead, including my parents, but I wanted to window shop a little longer. What a treat to look at the colorful displays and all the wonderful merchandise so beautifully displayed. It had been two years since I had seen anything like this. I lingered, looking at the **mannequins** with their glamorous dresses and stylish shoes, the sparkly jewelry in gold and silver, and the handsome living room and bedroom furniture. I longed for some of that beauty for myself.

As I strolled along, I noticed a barbershop nearby with the traditional revolving red, white and blue barber pole. There was a sign in the window that declared, "No Japs Allowed!" I glanced at a man in a white smock whom I assumed was a barber. He leaned against the doorframe, scowling. His jaws clenched and his lips pressed tighter together as he watched the bus passengers walk past his shop.

As I walked past the barber, a little ways behind the group, he bolted toward me. He grabbed me around the neck and pulled my head back against his chest with his left arm while pressing what I thought was a straight-edged razor against my throat with his right hand.

The spittle flew from his lips as he hissed in my ear, "I oughta slit your throat from ear to ear you goddam Jap!"

I froze. Blood pounded in my ears. My mind raced. *I am going to die.* I imagined blood spurting from my slit throat.

A split second later I felt a clear, impenetrable crystal ball totally encase me. It was as if I were inside of it, yet not inside of it. I didn't know where it came from or how it happened. All I knew was I could hear and see what was happening, terrified, yet strangely calm. The man's thick muscular arm around my neck cut off my breath. I felt cold and faint but stood perfectly still, waiting for his next move.

Just as abruptly, he released me with a grunt and a jarring shove as he growled under his breath, disgusted, "Get outta here, you goddam Jap." A man's voice somewhere in the distance yelled, "Hey, Ken, knock it off," followed by loud laughter.

I felt myself falling. I stretched out my arms, took several giant, staggering steps and regained my balance. *Don't fall*, I told myself, my legs like soft rubber. I took several more lurching steps, vigorously rubbing my neck and taking long, deep breaths. I stumbled away as quickly as I could.

Finally, I caught up with my folks just as Mama-san looked around to see if I was following. My breathing was slower by this time. My racing heart had slowed down. I was glad they had been far enough ahead and so engrossed with the sights and conversation that they did not see what had happened to me. Together, we walked back to the bus stop. I hid my terror and I *never* mentioned the incident.

Something deep inside of me resisted sharing that horrifying experience with my parents. I was beginning to feel more like an adult, and I wanted to act like one. I could deal with racism and protect them from one more assault, just as they had shielded me for many years.

~◎~

Two hours later, we arrived at the Minidoka Relocation Center, which was like all the other internment camps. My parents were assigned to one of the small living spaces for two people on the end of one of the barracks: 24-5-A. It was about 20'x12'. I was relieved to see several people from Vashon near them and was particularly pleased knowing the Umani family was only a few hours away.

I stayed at Minidoka for about a month, just long enough to be sure they were settled. My departure was nothing like it was for Yoneichi. We all knew where I was going and we all knew I could come "home" during school breaks.

The night before I left, I had trouble sleeping. I had never been away from my family, and I was going a long distance. I tried to imagine what it would be like living among strangers with demands on my time and intelligence.

The unknown worried me. *Will I measure up?* I wondered. *What if I don't? What if I get sick? And what if other white men grab me by the throat and put a razor to me?*

I shuddered at the memory of the Idaho incident. *Mama-san won't be there to take care of me. What will I do?* I began counting questions like sheep and finally dropped off to a troubled sleep.

⊰◉⊱

After breakfast in the mess hall, Mama-san and Papa-san accompanied me to the gate where a bus waited to take me to the train. Before I got on, Mama-san said, "Study hard and be mindful of your health." I put my arms across her shoulders and gave her a squeeze.

Then I shook Papa-san's hand as he said, "We're counting on you to become a very good nurse." I tried to smile and present a cheerful face, but the tears won out. "I promise I'll write," I said tearfully, then boarded the bus. After two years and three months confined to internment camps, I was finally leaving.

I left Minidoka in late August 1944, and traveled by train to Clinton, Iowa. It was a long and lonely trip. Mama-san made sure I had enough food with me so I wouldn't have to go to the diner. For three days I ate peanut butter and jelly sandwiches, carrot sticks, and cookies, and drank water I brought from the camp kitchen. For hours, I stared out the window, eating, thinking, and dreaming.

Life on the "outside" seemed both scary and exciting. At last, I was moving on with my life. Already I missed my parents and

Yoneichi, but I was also intrigued with my dream of becoming a nurse.

As the train carried me farther and farther away from the horrors of internment camp life, I felt myself lulled into a dream state. Everything was a feast to my eyes. I was mesmerized by the changing landscape—rolling hills, green grass, flowers and trees, people in cars driving along winding roads, and rivers meandering beside the railroad tracks.

I am going as a free person, I thought. I looked around at the other passengers and noted with a start, *These are all white people.* Everyone seemed preoccupied with his or her own issues and paid no attention to me. I reassured myself, *I can dismiss any fears about another experience like the one with the barber.*

When I arrived in Clinton, Iowa, Janet Sasaki was at the train station to greet me. I was relieved to see her familiar face. We caught the city transit bus and rode to the Jane Lamb Memorial Hospital. It was a 100-bed, four-story hospital and nurses' home. The large, red brick building was situated on a slight bluff with an imposing entryway.

We walked to the nurses' home where I would be living. It was a white, three-story, box-like building not far from the hospital. A covered walkway connected the nurses' home to the hospital. During my three-year training, there would be many times that I would run through that walkway in the middle of the night to assist with emergency surgery or the delivery of a baby.

The large, sedate sitting room in the nurses' home had a high ceiling and big windows that overlooked a sloping front lawn. The housemother, Mrs. Morrison, took us upstairs to the third floor and showed me my room.

After she left, I said to Janet, "Wow! A whole room to myself! After what we've been through, this looks like a palace." I didn't know what to expect, but this was a wonderful beginning as I started my nurses' training in the Midwest.

~CHAPTER TWENTY-TWO~

GOING OUR OWN WAYS

In the days that followed my departure, my parents went through the monotonous routine of camp life, eating meals in the mess hall, doing chores, engaging in idle chitchat with others. In between those activities, Mama-san was preoccupied and struggled to fill her days meaningfully. Later, in a letter Papa-san told me about an incident that prompted her to make a big change.

One day when Mama-san was in the laundry room, Mrs. Ohashi, a friend from Vashon, arrived. She said to Mama-san, "I heard that Yoneichi-san has gone into the service. Have you heard from him?"

"Oh, yes," Mama-san replied with quiet pride. "We got a letter from him last week telling us about his training."

"I'm surprised you let him go," Mrs. Ohashi said smugly. "My three sons are going to college in the Midwest."

Mama-san stiffened slightly. "We felt it was important to show our loyalty," she said defensively. "Yoneichi felt it was the right thing to do." She turned her head and looked at Mrs. Ohashi guardedly.

"But he's your only son, he could be killed," Mrs. Ohashi continued. "Then what would you do?" She shook her head with mock exasperation. "And now your daughter could end up going, too. How could you let both of them go? I would never let my children risk their lives for a country that's doing this to us."

Internees worked in fields at Minidoka Internment Camp in 1943, growing their own crops.

Mama-san stared at her, astonished. She quickly finished her laundry and returned to her room. Mama-san put away the clothes angrily, then sat down on her cot to think about what this "friend" had said to her. When Papa-san returned, he noticed that she seemed especially quiet and troubled.

Mama-san explained what had happened. Then she stood up and began pacing the floor, wringing her hands. As she paced back and forth, Papa-san saw how agitated and disturbed she was. He led her back to the cot and sat down opposite her. "That was a terrible thing for her to say to you!" he said. "What would you like me to do about it?"

After a moment, Mama-san asked, "Did we do the right thing?"

Papa-san was firm. "Of course we did. You remember our family discussion about this matter. Mrs. Ohashi was wrong to say those things to you, but you and I know that our children have done the right thing."

Still, Mama-san remained troubled. With her two children gone, she suddenly found herself without a meaningful role. Everything she had done since her arrival in this country was as our mother and our protector. For the first time since our evacuation, the pressures of camp life had become too much for Mama-san.

My parents discussed their possibilities. Mama-san wondered about leaving camp for some temporary work outside, and decided that it would be good to get away, even for a short period of time. They went to the administration building and learned that openings were available at a vegetable-canning factory in Ogden, Utah. Mama-san shared the idea with Ochiyo-san, a distant relative who also lived in Minidoka, and asked her if she would like to go with her. Ochiyo-san thought the idea was a good one. Both of them applied for leave and received it promptly.

Papa-san fully understood Mama-san's need to get away, but they decided that he needed to remain in camp to serve as a focal point for all of us. He was not bothered by mean-spirited comments, so staying in camp was no special hardship. He felt strongly that Mama-san should take a break away from the stress that threatened to overwhelm her and do something that would be renewing for her.

WING LUKE MUSEUM

Women scrubbed their laundry in washtubs in the camp laundry room. This is where women often visited as they worked.

Papa-san wrote several letters to me explaining Mama-san's plans. I understood and was glad that she would be getting out of camp for a while.

⊙

Not long after Mama-san left for Ogden, Utah, she wrote me a short letter dated September 3, 1944:

The cannery doesn't seem to be very big but it seems good. We will begin working from Monday morning. Four of us women are in the same room. Ochiyo-san and Ohide-san will go to another place in two evenings from now. Mrs. Yamaguchi-san and I will stay here. She is a very fine person. There aren't enough workers yet.

The cannery is beside some woods near a mountain. It is very quiet and it feels very good to be here. Please be sure and take care of your body. Mama.

This was the first time, to my knowledge, that Mama-san had done something away from the family for her own well being. It told me a lot about how much stress she had been hiding from us. To be with other fine women in a quiet, peaceful environment near trees and mountains must have felt like heaven after two years of the congested, noisy, dusty camps.

This made me think about how much stress and grief Mama-san had endured for most of her life—beginning when she was very young. Several years earlier Mama-san had told me about her parents while we washed dishes on the farm.

"I don't remember much about my father because he died when I was two years old," Mama-san explained.

With a faraway look on her face she continued, "But I was six when my mother died. My mother must have been very ill because she stayed in bed for days. That was not like her at all. Whenever I went in to see her and asked her why she was still in bed, she'd apologize for being so lazy and put me off with some excuse.

"One day a lot of people came to our home. Some came to help clean the house, others to cook extra food. It was all very confusing. My oldest sister, Chizuko, took me aside and tearfully told me that our mother had died, but I didn't understand what that meant.

"I kept opening the *shoji* panel door to the room where my mother slept, but she was not there. I looked among the *futon* comforters piled in the storage cupboard hoping to find her there, but she wasn't there either.

"Weeks later, I finally realized that my mother would not be with us any more. I went looking for Chizuko-san to ask her. She took me in her arms and rocked me back and forth, back and forth. I cried and cried, and even now, when I think about it, I feel sad for that little girl so long ago, longing for her mother."

◦❀◦

In mid-September, Mama-san wrote again, telling me how much she enjoyed being out of the internment camp, making friends with other Japanese-American women at the canning factory, and working hard every day.

"When I work I forget about everything else," wrote Mama-san. "I don't even worry about Yoneichi-san. I don't know how it is, but I can work with a happy heart here. I think it comes from God."

Mama-san's desire to remain in Ogden was understandable. I was deeply grateful that this could be so. During this critical time, Papa-san provided the stability we all needed. Papa-san clearly understood Mama-san's fragility at this time and willingly gave her the space she needed in which to regain her strong spirit, which had become so frayed. I saw this as the most powerful evidence of Papa-san's love for his wife. In spite of the traditional subservient role that many Japanese women followed, Papa-san honored his wife's need to seek change.

I was often too exhausted to write letters on a regular basis to my parents, but my letters were very important to them. Mama-san wrote to me often, but I was not so good at replying promptly. Papa-san knew how much my letters meant to Mama-san, so he wrote to me encouraging me to write more often.

In his letter to me on November 23, 1944, Papa-san wrote in part:

I think our Mama-san with her acquaintance with suffering is the greatest person. Mary-san, you must be very thankful for her. Write her about that. Mama-san will be very pleased about that.

Even though they may be short, please write one letter per week to your Mama-san. I repeat myself. Even if it's short, please be sure to write to Mama-san every week. I ask you to do that for her.
Papa

I could tell from this letter that Papa-san was very aware of Mama-san's struggle. This was the tender loving part of Papa-san's character. I promptly wrote to thank and commend him for his support of Mama-san.

When Mama-san wrote to me from Utah, she sounded like her own self again. Her letters, written in Japanese, were filled with her concerns for my health as well as her delight with a photograph Yoneichi had sent her.

Mama-san often reminded me to pay attention to my body. In one letter, she mentioned that if I neglect my body and skimp on nourishing food, the body could get worn down and I would not be able to study hard and care for the patients in the hospital.

∗◎∗

In the fall of 1944, each of us faced ongoing internal challenges while the world outside seemed turbulent, frightful, and unresolved. Yoneichi was in basic training at Camp Blanding, Florida. Mama-san was sorting peas in a vegetable canning factory in Ogden, Utah. I was engrossed in my nursing studies in Clinton, Iowa. And Papa-san was the center for all of us at "home" in Minidoka Internment Camp.

While away, Mama-san regained her perspective on her family and the world. Her letters were full of encouragement and faith that all of this would pass and we would come back together once again. We felt connected to each other, informed, and loved in spite of the distances and issues that pressed upon each of us. We would all need to gather our strength for the trials that lay ahead.

CHAPTER TWENTY-THREE

ON MY OWN

Our family was reunited for a brief time at Minidoka the end of December 1944. Yoneichi had spent six months in basic training, and was allowed a short farewell visit before going overseas. I also got a short leave from nursing school over the holidays.

Before arriving at Minidoka, Yoneichi visited Vashon to check on our farm for a few hours. This was a risky thing for him to do since Japanese were still officially restricted from the West Coast. Yoneichi reported that the farm seemed run down but otherwise okay. Mack was nowhere to be found, which was not surprising, considering it was the Christmas season.

I was feeling a bit self-conscious about visiting the internment camp in my nurse's uniform. I wore a soft gray suit and topcoat, both with red epaulets, which are fancy shoulder pieces on uniforms. On my head I wore a special cap as a member of the United States Cadet Nurse Corps.

When I arrived, the internment camp no longer seemed as threatening and confining with its guardhouse and armed soldiers. When I first saw Yoneichi, I thought, *He sure looks handsome in that khaki uniform of the United States Army.* But I also realized with a sharp attack of panic, *That uniform could kill him.*

When we went to the mess hall for dinner that December evening, people stared at us. I whispered to Mama-san, "Aren't

Mary and Yoneichi in uniform at Minidoka before Yoneichi left for combat in Europe in 1944.

these people used to seeing young people in uniform by now?"

She smiled and replied, "They're used to seeing more and more men in uniform, but I think you are the first woman."

I shrugged my shoulders and smiled. What mattered most was being with family again. We caught up on the news of one another's lives, talked about new and old friends, and recalled fond memories of our years on the farm.

Our precious days together slipped away like ice cream on a hot day. Before we knew it, and before we were ready, it was time to leave. This time it seemed harder for Mama-san to watch us approach the bus, but seeing us together seemed to give her some comfort.

I shook Papa-san's hand and held it longer than usual. Spontaneously, I gave Mama-san a big, long, bear hug. We rarely hugged or kissed in our family; it was not customary among the Japanese. Bowing was the custom, but this was no ordinary good-bye.

"Try not to worry, Mama-san. We must trust God to help us through this," I said as much to myself as to her.

Yoneichi took Mama-san into his arms, too, and held her for a long time. This was the first time I had seen him do that. "I'll be careful. Try not to worry, Mama-san," Yoneichi said, holding her as if he might not see her again.

She nodded through her tears as she said, *"Ochitsuite yo."* (Be calm, self-possessed.)

Yoneichi nodded and reluctantly let go. Then he gave Papa-san a firm handshake. Both of their eyes were moist. Then it was time to go. We both boarded the bus and waved to our parents as they watched with brave smiles on their sad faces.

We caught the train in Pocatello, Idaho, and rode together heading east. We were both quiet for the first hour or so. This was one of the few times when the two of us were alone together. I wondered, *Will this be our last time together?*

Finally, I said, "You said to our folks that you didn't see the deputy sheriff when you went to Vashon to see the farm and that you hadn't heard from him either. Don't you think we should have heard from him by now?"

"I don't know what's going on with him," Yoneichi responded. "Why don't you write and ask him to send the statements for the past three years to you instead of to me. He should have them by this time."

"And if he doesn't?" I asked.

Yoneichi thought a bit, then replied, "There isn't a lot we can do from where we are. You could write to the Administration Office at Minidoka and see if they have people there who could help. But at this point, just wait a little while and see what happens."

Before I got off the train at Clinton, I gave my brother a big hug and said, "I'll be thinking of you every day. Bye, and be careful."

As the train pulled away from the station, I stood waving a long time until the train disappeared. An emptiness settled into my chest as I raised a silent prayer on his behalf.

~◎~

Yoneichi traveled to the East Coast to join the rest of his group at Fort George Meade in Maryland. For the next couple of weeks, he learned to use different weapons. Then he and the other men gathered at the Assembly Center at Camp Killmer, New Jersey and boarded a freighter for a nineteen-day journey across the Atlantic Ocean. They landed at Marseilles in southern France and were assigned to the 442nd Regimental Combat Team.

At that time, the United States military forces were fully involved in fierce battles in Europe and in the South Pacific. Things were difficult at home, too. I heard from a former classmate, Angie, on Vashon:

> We are all participating in blackouts and civil defense drills now. Consumer goods like refrigerators are harder to buy because factories have converted to war production. All kinds of supplies are now rationed, including gasoline, tires, coffee, sugar, meat and shoes.

> We received ration cards for these items and we can use them only for a given period of time and only if the local store has the product. There was a call for skilled workers to work in defense jobs. I am planning to apply for some kind of work at Boeing [a major aircraft manufacturer that made bombers for the war].

Many women left their homes for the first time and stepped into the work force. They took factory jobs once held by men who went overseas to fight. "Rosie the Riveter" became a common phrase, a symbol of hard-working women in factories during World War II.

It was hard for me to feel at home in Iowa, especially because I stood out as one of the first Asians in Clinton. One day, when I was on the bus, I noticed a couple of white women sitting across the aisle on a seat facing me. They were whispering to each other and glancing at me. I looked away, but whenever I glanced back, they were still talking and staring at me.

Finally, I thought to myself, *That's enough. I can stare too.* I frowned and stared back. They quickly looked away and before long got off the bus.

Fortunately, I had become close friends with one of my classmates, Ellen Evans, and I visited her home on many occasions. I felt included and loved like another daughter in Ellen's family. This brought me great comfort.

~⑥~

In late February, Mama-san wrote me a letter, worried because she had not heard from Yoneichi. She was worried because she had a vivid dream about him. Mama-san also mentioned that one of the Japanese homes on Vashon Island had burned a week earlier around midnight.

Mama-san's letter was chilling. I hadn't heard from Yoneichi either. That night I stayed on my knees beside my bed a long time lifting prayer after prayer to God for strength and comfort for all who suffered because of this terrible war.

And what about the house burning on Vashon? Did someone deliberately set that fire? I later learned three Japanese families had stored all of their personal belongings in that house before they were evacuated. Now, they would have nothing from their former lives. In the midst of my sleepless night, it suddenly occurred to me that the same thing could happen to our house on Vashon.

While Yoneichi was never far from my thoughts, I had to devote my full attention to nursing school. There were few registered nurses in civilian hospitals since many were in the military. We students filled in the gaps. There were times when I put in fourteen-hour days, working double shifts to cover patient needs. Often, I was on call for twenty-four hours at a time for emergencies.

One of my favorite classes was dietetics, studying nutrition and learning about special dietary needs of patients hospitalized with specific types of disease. Our teacher was a young, vivacious woman named Mrs. Heidinger.

One day, I was called to the Director of Nurses office. Mrs. Heidinger was there, too. Miss Rinehart, the director, told me that Mrs. Heidinger was returning to her home in Illinois and she recommended me to make up the menus and prepare the trays for patients who needed special diets.

I was surprised they chose me for this responsible position. Immediately, my self-respect and my faith in America began to be restored. I enthusiastically accepted the offer.

I plunged into my new work, reading everything I could find on various diets, including those for diabetes, ulcers, and gall bladder difficulties. Many of the patients' diets required great care—fat, protein, carbohydrates, and other dietary requirements had to be calculated precisely for each patient. I especially paid attention to the way the trays were made up so they looked appetizing. It was one of my most satisfying times as a student.

⚛

In mid-March 1945, Mama-san wrote saying letters were arriving from creditors requesting payments for fertilizer, plants, labor, and other costs associated with running the farm. I was stunned. Based on the contract that Yoneichi and the deputy sheriff had signed prior to our evacuation, the deputy sheriff was supposed to handle all of these details. The contract stated that expenses and income would be split 50/50 between the deputy sheriff and us.

It was clear to us that this was not happening. The deputy sheriff had apparently pocketed the profits, and failed to pay the expenses. I had no money to pay those bills, Yoneichi was overseas, and my parents were aliens with no civil rights. Before long, I would have to spend a great deal of time and energy helping my parents figure out this situation.

In December 1944, the government **rescinded** Executive Order 9066, which had ordered the evacuation of all Japanese and Japanese Americans from the West Coast in 1942. Now, many internees faced a new problem. Where would they go if they no longer had their homes?

Many Japanese Americans had lost their homes and their farms. The fathers of many families who had lived on Terminal Island in Southern California had been arrested and the government had seized their fishing boats. What about the business people throughout the Western states whose previous livelihoods had to be left behind? How would they support themselves with no assets? If foreign-born parents, the *Isseis*, had sons in the service and they were killed, how could the parents provide for themselves when they had no civil rights?

Whatever the circumstances, news of the internment camps closing caused alarm and severe agitation among all the internees. They had become accustomed to enforced idleness and dependent upon the government for their food and shelter. Now, they faced the reality that all of this would evaporate in the near future. Although most of the Japanese Americans wanted to return to the West Coast where they had lived and worked since their arrival in the United States, the memory still lingered of severe prejudice that forced them out.

In her letter on April 1, 1945, Mama-san explained their dilemma:

Papa-san is not a citizen and without you around and without a legal authorization from you, he cannot sell the produce nor pay the people who work for us. This is true for California, Oregon and Washington only, I think. That is because of this complicated law.

If you [Mary] were with us, then Papa-san could do the work and there wouldn't be any trouble. Until Yoneichi-san returns you are the boss and the boss isn't here with the land document. We can't do a thing. Therefore, you have to ask a lawyer to make this letter of authority so you can entrust Papa-san to do the work for you. The WRA showed us how this is to be done. When you have completed the document, please send it to us.

The WRA placed a collection notice on Deputy Sheriff Hopkins, but we haven't heard a thing yet. Thank you for taking care of this for us.
Mama

I was shocked to read this letter. *I can't do all this on top of everything else I have to do in nurses' training,* I thought. *Where would I begin?*

Mama-san and Papa-san were reasonably sure they had the farm to return to, but at the time of the evacuation they didn't realize that Yoneichi and I would not be going back with them. Before they left for Vashon, they had to have this legal document.

While we were trying to solve this problem, many dozens of frantic letters flew back and forth between my parents and me trying to figure out how to get this done. Telephones were not available in camp, making communication much slower.

Mama-san always wrote in Japanese and there were times when I had difficulty translating certain characters. It was agonizing to read and write in Japanese when my thoughts were in English. To makes things worse, my parents wanted me to do things, but they didn't always know specifically what it was they needed me to do.

Because I was twenty years old and inexperienced with no college education, and no training in law or finances, I was terribly frustrated. But I knew I had to help my parents.

The problem got even more complicated and perplexing. First, I wrote a letter to the deputy sheriff and requested reports for the years since our departure. His response was slow to arrive; then he wrote that he had sent them to Yoneichi. Without Yoneichi to ask, we wondered where (or whether) the deputy sheriff really sent them. We finally began to doubt that the deputy sheriff had sent any of the reports for 1942, 1943, or 1944. We suspected he kept all the checks for the strawberries and paid only minimal expenses, leaving major debts for us to deal with later.

Another thing bothered me. Why didn't we hear from Mack, the man whom we entrusted to actually work on the property? Could he give us any clues about what was going on back home?

While handling all these problems on the farm, I also worked extended hours at the hospital. Often, I lay awake at night wondering what to do.

Less than two weeks after the letter from Mama-san arrived, I got a letter from Papa-san. He acknowledged how busy I must be with school, but he also reminded me that it was my responsibility to help

Mary in 1944.

them in Yoneichi's absence. I needed to seek some legal help to straighten out the farm situation.

One day, I worked up my courage and went to a lawyer in Clinton. Tense and nervous, I explained our situation and then asked for his assistance.

The lawyer paused for quite a while as he shuffled papers back and forth on his desk as he thought about my request. Finally, he looked up, frowned, and said, "You're asking me to take on a deputy sheriff *and* the United States government in a dispute happening 2,000 miles away? Good luck, but frankly, I can't help you." He turned away in his chair. It was obvious this was the end of the conversation.

While I had braced myself for this kind of response, I still felt my face flush and my muscles tighten. Maybe he was reluctant to deal with a huge federal bureaucracy, or maybe he was prejudiced and just didn't want to get involved with a Jap. The trouble was, he was the only lawyer in town.

After I got back to the nurses' home, I paced in my room, clenching and unclenching my fists as tears of frustration and anger rushed through me. Finally, I sat down to write a disappointing letter to my parents.

As I stared out the window with my arms across my chest, pen in hand, I felt overwhelmed and resentful. Suddenly, Yoneichi's face appeared before me and I heard his words: "Take good care of the folks. You know how important that is to me. It's up to you now, you know."

I stopped frowning and realized this was something I *must* do. It was my responsibility and my privilege to do it for Yoneichi, for our parents, and for me. This was the Japanese value of *on*—a sense of loyalty, respect, and gratitude toward one's parents.

CHAPTER TWENTY-FOUR

NISEI SOLDIERS

Yoneichi never talked about his wartime experiences with any of us. Many soldiers do not talk in detail about their involvement in war—except among themselves. The *Nisei* soldiers seemed especially reluctant to discuss their experiences during World War II—even decades later.

For several years after the War, I asked Yoneichi about some of his experiences, but he would always look away and say, "I'll tell you about it some other time." Unfortunately, that time never came. Maybe he didn't talk about his war experiences as a way to protect others, or perhaps to protect himself. Maybe he had to kill other people—he never said, and I never asked. Maybe close friends of his were injured or killed. He never said and I never asked.

Years later, while writing this book, I had to search for my brother's story. Along with books from the library, I learned about the courageous stories of the Japanese-American soldiers of the 100th / 442nd Regimental Combat Team from Yoneichi's friends who fought in the war. There was one friend in particular who had been a classmate of Yoneichi's in high school and they had fought in Italy at the same time. I met with this man many times and he shared his memories, books, and various papers to give me more specific information.

Initially, the 100th Battalion was made up of all Japanese-American volunteers from Hawaii, which was a U.S. territory during World War II. (Hawaii became the fiftieth state in 1959.) Thousands of Japanese-American men volunteered, many more than the army expected.

Their outstanding success fighting battles in North Africa and Italy confirmed to U.S. military leadership how valuable the Japanese-American soldiers could be. By the time the first large group of *Niseis* from the United States mainland arrived in Europe in early 1945, the men of the 100th Battalion had distinguished themselves through months of rugged fighting. The embattled soldiers retained their special identification as the 100th Battalion in recognition of their combat record.

The newly arrived Japanese-American soldiers replaced many of the soldiers in the 100th Battalion who had died. Then, they joined with the 2nd and 3rd Battalions to make up the 442nd Regimental Combat Team. When Yoneichi arrived in early 1945, he was assigned to Company G of the 2nd Battalion.

The reputation of the *Nisei* fighting spirit was both a blessing and a curse. It was a blessing because it proved the loyalty of Japanese-American soldiers beyond a shadow of a doubt. It was also a curse because the *Nisei* soldiers got the deadliest assignments and many of them died in battle. The fear among Japanese-American families was that our men could be sacrificed to meet military goals and could be sent on the most dangerous missions on the frontline, often facing impossible odds.

I read many books about the men of the 100th/442nd, wanting to understand what my brother endured. I wept as I read accounts of the high price Japanese-American soldiers paid to rescue "The Lost Battalion" in five days of battle. About 200 soldiers in the 100th/442nd Regimental Combat Team were killed, and about 800 others seriously wounded while rescuing 211 U.S. soldiers from Texas who were surrounded by German forces.

Here was the evidence that I feared—the Japanese-American

soldiers were dedicated to giving their all, knowing they could be considered dispensable. I wondered, *Was this the bias that Yoneichi could never speak of?* I would never know for certain. I knew *Nisei* men like Yoneichi were determined to fight hard to prove their loyalty to the United States.

Once Yoneichi went overseas, he wrote infrequently. When he did write, my parents always promptly relayed his updates to me in Iowa. He wrote only in generalities, such as, "I am *genki* (in high spirit, vigorous). How are you? I hope all is well with all of you."

Yoneichi chose his words carefully. They did not reflect the horrors of the war he was fighting in France and Italy. In those days of censorship and war secrets, Yoneichi would not have been allowed to tell us much even if he had wanted to.

In early 1945, the 100th/442nd battalion joined with the 5th Army for a crucial military campaign that included several Ally countries. Yoneichi became a part of this unit and participated in the major battle that was to follow.

THE NATIONAL ARCHIVES

A Group of 100th Infantry Battalion soldiers.

For years, I could only imagine how bad it was for my brother—he never told us. Only once in a letter to Mama-san did Yoneichi mention any of the fierce fighting. He simply wrote, "Some of the bullets came pretty close." That was it.

After the backbone of the Nazi German Army—the Gothic Line—had been broken in Italy, Yoneichi's letters began arriving weekly. A letter from Yoneichi was always wonderful—we knew he was alive!

⊰◉⊱

While the battles in Europe raged with *Nisei* soldiers bravely fighting as loyal Americans, there was another group of *Nisei* soldiers fighting in the South Pacific against Japan. About 5,000 Japanese-American men were a part of the Military Intelligence Service (MIS). These *Nisei* soldiers trained for **counter-intelligence** because they spoke and read both English and Japanese. They could interrogate Japanese prisoners of war, and translate Japanese maps, documents and radio transmissions. The MIS *Nisei* **linguists** served in almost every major battle in the Pacific during World War II.

During the War, few people knew about the secret missions of the MIS *Nisei* soldiers. They were under tight security wraps because they could be killed by enemy fire as well as **"friendly fire"** because they looked like the enemy. These *Nisei* soldiers were called the "eyes and ears" of every command.

For decades after the War, the secret nature of the MIS soldiers' work was kept as **"classified."** It would be many years later before the general public knew about the bravery of the MIS *Nisei* soldiers. The military estimates that these Japanese-American soldiers secretly saved countless Allied lives and shortened World War II by two years. Finally, more than fifty years after World War II, the MIS soldiers received the Presidential Unit Citation in April 2000 for their wartime contributions.

⊰◉⊱

The combined 100th and the 442nd Regimental Combat Team became known as the "Go For Broke" Regiment. They fought fiercely and suffered dearly.

For its relatively small size, the "Go for Broke" regiment was the most highly decorated unit in the history of the United States Armed Forces, which includes the Army, Navy, Marine Corps, Air Force, and Coast Guard. Over the course of World War II, about 18,500 soldiers served in the 100th/442nd. The unit earned more than 18,000 individual decorations, including 9,486 Purple Hearts. The 100th/442nd Regimental Combat Team was nicknamed "The Purple Heart Battalion" in recognition of all the medals the soldiers earned.

The soldiers of the 100th/442nd unit also earned seven Presidential Unit Citations, the nation's top award for combat units. When they received the seventh presidential citation, they were the only military unit returning from overseas battlefields to have the honor of being reviewed by President Harry S Truman. Yoneichi was a part of that unit, but chose to miss this special military honor in order to quickly return home to help our parents on the farm.

When I heard about the honors received by the *Nisei* fighting men, I was very proud. It was not until decades later that most people would learn of the heroism and sacrifice of the *Nisei* soldiers.

Yoneichi in 1944.

In fact, it would be decades later that I would learn that Yoneichi had received a Bronze Star for "distinguishing himself by heroic or meritorious achievement...in connection with military operations against an armed enemy on or about 20 April 1945."

None of us will ever know what Yoneichi did to earn that medal; he never mentioned it. I learned about it from Yoneichi's widow, who found his Bronze Star among his wartime memorabilia after his death.

Although I am not surprised that Yoneichi did not talk about his Bronze Star, how I wish I had known about it. I would have expressed my deep gratitude and pride in Yoneichi's unselfish service to our people and the United States.

Like most of the *Nisei* men who went to war, Yoneichi did not want to take credit for what he had done. It is part of the Japanese culture to always be modest, and never brag about our successes. "I was one of many" was a statement commonly made by the Japanese-American men who fought in the war. Yoneichi felt the same way.

I am certain Yoneichi suffered a great deal of anguish about the war, no different from any other soldier who lost his best friends in combat. On top of everything else, Yoneichi was a religious person, and the idea of killing others, even in a "just" war, was philosophically unacceptable to him. He had to go and fight, and every day face the possibility of his own death.

◈

Years later, historians as well as politicians would attribute the outstanding record of the 100th and 442nd battalions as influential factors in the U.S. decision to confirm the statehood of Hawaii in 1959. Many of the *Nisei* soldiers in the 100th/442nd battalions were from Hawaii.

I believe another major benefit that resulted from the struggles of the war years is the change in Japanese-American status in our country. Instead of working primarily at low-paying, menial jobs, they had opportunities for positions in the professions and management.

After the war, Japanese Americans became teachers, university professors, lawyers, dentists, doctors—whatever they chose to do was open to them. Many used their G.I. Bill—government benefits for veterans attending college or vocational training—to pay for college tuition, and went on to become professionals in their chosen fields. This is what Yoneichi did.

The future for Japanese Americans had changed profoundly, and I would never forget the courage of Yoneichi and the *Nisei* soldiers.

Army soldiers from the 306th Headquarters Intelligence Detachment, XXIV Corps, served in the Military Intelligence Service (MIS). They translated captured Japanese documents that gave U.S. forces a big advantage in winning the war in the Pacific. Technical Sergeant Michio Tsuneishi (front row, right) shared his story and photos online at the Library of Congress's "Veterans' History Project." While Tsuneishi served in the U.S. Army, his family was confined at Heart Mountain Internment Camp.

CHAPTER TWENTY-FIVE

THE WAR ENDS

After months of seemingly slow progress, the War turned rapidly. In a matter of days, stunning news signaled the end of the War in Europe.

On April 27, 1945 the dictator of Italy, Benito Mussolini, was captured, and the next day executed. Two days later, Germany's Nazi dictator, Adolf Hitler, committed suicide once he realized the War was lost. Four days later German forces in Italy surrendered, followed by German forces surrendering throughout Europe.

Americans awoke May 8th to the news of Nazi Germany's complete surrender, which was declared "V-E Day" (Victory in Europe Day). When I read about this incredible news, I was in the nurses' lounge relaxing. Immediately, a dam of emotions broke inside of me. I rushed upstairs to my room, fell on my knees by my bed, and tearfully thanked God. *The war is finally over*, I told myself, sobbing. *Our family will be together again.*

Repeatedly, I reassured myself, *Yoneichi will be safe, alive, uninjured.*

Things were improving in other ways, too. As Mama-san and Papa-san requested, I had written letters to the War Relocation Authority offices in Chicago, Illinois; Des Moines, Iowa; and Tacoma, Washington. I appealed for help with the ownership of the farm. I knew we were not the only ones needing assistance.

In the meantime, my parents finally found a lawyer in the social service department at Minidoka camp willing to help untangle our situation. The lawyer sent a letter to several creditors requesting a postponement of debt payments until we could get our legal issues straightened out or until Yoneichi returned from the War. They soon received replies saying this would be acceptable.

⊰◉⊱

The World War II battles in the Pacific with Japan continued. At the same time, U.S. scientists were secretly working on the first atomic bomb, a nuclear weapon capable of destroying whole cities. There had been tremendous fear that Nazi Germany was also trying to develop the first nuclear weapons.

In July 1945, the U.S. scientists developed and successfully tested an atomic bomb that was available to the Army. Now, it was up to President Harry S Truman as the Commander-in-Chief to decide whether or not to use the bomb against Japan. A little more than a week later, President Truman secretly made his decision with this new weapon of "unusual destructive force."

On the afternoon of August 7, after a full day at the hospital, I returned to my room to rest and prepare for classes the next day. In the downstairs lounge I picked up the local newspaper and saw the headlines:

FIRST ATOMIC BOMB DROPPED ON JAPAN; MISSILE IS EQUAL TO 20,000 TONS OF TNT; TRUMAN WARNS FOE OF A 'RAIN OF RUIN.'

An aerial photograph taken shortly after the bombing showed a huge mushroom cloud above the devastated city of Hiroshima, Japan. The United States had used its atomic power on August 6. It was the first time the public had ever heard of a weapon of mass destruction, and the United States had used it.

U.S. GOVERNMENT, LIBRARY OF CONGRESS

View of Hiroshima City in Japan after the U.S. dropped an atomic bomb on August 6, 1945. The exact number of deaths caused by the bombing is uncertain, but it is estimated more than 100,000 people died that day.

The photos on the front page showed the total devastation of what was once a bustling city. The few remaining buildings in various stages of collapse stood out in sharp contrast to the dark, thick clouds of dust, smoke, and debris billowing into the sky.

The ground was littered with twisted, naked bodies, many burned and charred. Photos showed dazed people running or walking with scorched hair and skin hanging from their arms and legs. *The people in this picture are Japanese, just like me*, I thought as I stared at the photographs.

I had hated the Japanese government for its role in starting this war and thrusting me into a situation that resulted in my imprisonment. I was shocked at the aggressive and brutal way Japan treated its neighboring countries, both before and during the War. I was angry that Japan attacked Pearl Harbor, both for what it did to my country and to me personally. At the same time, when I saw the pictures of Japanese people in Japan burned and charred by the atomic blast, I was heartbroken for them. I was an American by birth, but at that moment, I was Japanese.

As I looked at the pictures, I felt nauseous and dizzy, as if I had been hit in the head and stomach. So many innocent lives wiped out. I knew instantly that the United States had won the war.

My tears were a mix of relief and pain. Even though a part of me was glad the United States won the war, the Japanese part of me was speechless with grief and horror. I ran up to my room, fell on my bed, and sobbed.

A few minutes later, there was a soft knock on the door. My dearest classmate Ellen came in, sat on the bed beside me, gently put her arms around me, and held me close as we both cried.

That evening in the dining room, the usual lively conversations were subdued. A classmate came up to me, put her hands on my shoulders, and whispered into my ear, "I'm sorry, Mary."

The others hovered near, but were silent. I could tell from their sad expressions that they didn't know what to say. I just nodded my head at each of them and said, "Thanks." Tears ran down my face.

Mama-san and Papa-san came to America by choice and stood by their decision against such terrible odds. However, I could imagine them staring silently at the internment camp newspaper, reading about the Bombing of Hiroshima. I knew they would be absolutely stunned by what they read. Japan was the land of their birth, still home to many of their relatives.

~ CHAPTER TWENTY-SIX ~

HOME AGAIN

The end of World War II became a time of great celebration around the country. We all hoped and prayed this would be the *last* world war. For more than six years, World War II raged, becoming the bloodiest war in history and spreading to nearly every part of the world.

For my family, the end of the War signaled the eventual end of Japanese-American internment and the closing of the camps. President Roosevelt had rescinded Executive Order 9066 in December 1944, but it took many months for the U.S. government to release internees and shut down the camps.

People still in the camps began leaving, most returning to the West Coast, even if they didn't have a home or a business to return to. For them, the West Coast of the United States was still considered home despite hardships and racism they had endured.

Mama-san wrote to let me know they would be leaving Minidoka on September 5, 1945. She ended her letter assuring me, "Don't worry about a thing."

I later realized there were many things still unresolved. Although Mama-san sounded optimistic, I imagined she was filled with both eagerness and fear. I felt similarly, and wanted to return with my parents, but I had to finish my nurse's training.

My parents left Minidoka internment camp with $25 each from the U.S. government for travel expenses. Two days later they arrived home. In a letter, Mama-san wrote, "The piano is here. The house doesn't look too bad. The strawberries look good. We have two acres."

My parents were engrossed in cleaning up the house and getting the yard in order. From our farm, Mama-san wrote on September 14:

It is now one week since we got home. Every day, every day, I am cleaning the house. Mack has taken care of it fairly well, so Papa-san and I are rejoicing. He painted the house. It looks fine.

Mrs. Peterson and Mrs. McDonald brought a lot of vegetables. They're delicious. Our feelings are better than we had hoped. The strawberry plants are growing well.

There are more Japanese people coming back to Vashon. They will come and stay at our place until they can find a place to live. It is wonderful, isn't it?

The white people on Vashon, all of them, are very nice to us. Rejoice with us! Mama.

I did rejoice! It was better than I could have imagined. My parents returned in September, so the following year's crop would belong to them, according to the contract with the deputy sheriff. However, my parents still had to deal with the creditors and the deputy sheriff's poor bookkeeping. They decided to wait until Yoneichi returned from Europe to resolve the financial problems.

I suspected Mama-san's mixed feelings about returning home were shared by the majority of *Isseis* who planned to return to the West Coast. Many could not forget the terrible injustices done to them prior to their imprisonment in internment camps. They feared resistance when they tried to return to their former homes.

For those in California whose homes or businesses were already lost, their feelings of dread and fear were probably far more extreme. In some cases, those feelings turned out to be well justified. Returning home was painful and difficult for many Japanese Americans. Years later, some of their stories would be told in the book, *Unlikely Liberators: The Men of the 100th and 442nd,* by Masayo Umezawa Duus. Two of those stories in particular haunted me when I read them.

In 1945, shortly after the end of the war in Europe, U.S. newspapers reported the tragic story of the family of Sergeant Kazuo Masuda. He was a *Nisei* hero who had been killed in northern Italy. When his family, the Masudas, tried to return to their home

General Stillwell presents the Masuda family with Sergeant Kazuo Masuda's Distinguished Service Cross. Mary Masuda (sister) in front, Masao Masuda in uniform on left, and parents, Mr. & Mrs. Gensuke Masuda.

in Santa Ana, California, after the war, the neighbors drove them away. Despite their dead son's heroic war efforts, the Southern California community did not welcome home the Masudas.

The situation would not change until six months later when General Joseph "Vinegar Joe" Stillwell, a war hero who fought in Asia, came to California on behalf of the military to honor the Masudas. The photograph of General Stillwell standing in front of the family's small wooden house, presenting Sergeant Masuda's Distinguished Service Cross to his family aroused the community's sympathy for the family.

Another painful story of racism against Japanese Americans after the end of the war took place in Hood River, Oregon. The local American Legion removed the names of sixteen Japanese-American soldiers from the honor roll in front of Hood River's city hall. This caused a national uproar. Faced with criticism from the American Legion's national headquarters and many other branches, the Hood River branch of the American Legion restored the names of the Japanese Americans on the honor roll.

Even though their sons had died in the war, proving their loyalty to the United States, Japanese-American families still faced post-war prejudice. Yet, these stories also demonstrated how the *Nisei* soldiers, through their persistent courage and loyalty, finally succeeded in winning acceptance from the general public.

It was important to me that Japanese Americans be respected, and it was satisfying when that began to happen. When the *Nisei* combat battalions' wartime sacrifices became legendary, I thought, *These incredible sacrifices have become the absolute proof of our loyalty to the United States.*

Now, I longed for a time when I could once again proudly be Japanese *and* American.

While the war had been unofficially over in Europe since May, the men were still doing guard duty in various places throughout Europe. Yoneichi wrote to Mama-san requesting Japanese pickles, *umeboshi* (sour plums), and *wasabi* (horseradish). He wanted foods that reminded him of home, especially for Christmas 1945 when he would still be thousands of miles away.

That Christmas I was lonely, too. It was a typical snowy Iowa winter, both wondrous and desolate. We had completed classes for the quarter and most of my classmates who lived in the area had gone home for the holidays. Patients needed care and I was one of the students who stayed at the hospital.

One of my patients was an older gentleman who owned a major department store in Clinton. His wife had died the previous year, and he was lonely. I took extra time with him, listening to his memories of years spent with his loving wife. He had many stories about the life they shared, their children, and how much he missed her. By listening to this man's sorrow and offering him comfort, I felt better myself.

A week later, I got a letter from Mama-san that she wrote on Christmas Day that made me feel loved and thought about:

Merry Christmas! The four of us had dinner together. I made a pie out of squash, made candied sweet potatoes, roast beef and baked biscuits.

Putting Yoneichi-san's and your pictures on your chairs, we conversed with you as we ate our dinner. It was a wonderful meal.

You couldn't come home for vacation so it must have been a very lonely Christmas. I think about that and feel apologetic but shikata ga nai (it can't be helped).

My parents were busy throughout the winter with mainte-nance work on the farm. I could imagine them buying food and essential items on credit from local grocers who had known them for years and trusted them. They purchased fertilizer and sup- plies with money advanced by the National Fruit Company, a company they had sold crops to for years before the war. My par- ents could also buy strawberry plants from the man who owned the Vashon Packing Company. They had little money to live on that winter, but they persisted despite the difficulties.

As spring 1946 came, my parents were anticipating Yoneichi's return from Europe, perhaps as early as that autumn. Mama-san sent me a letter describing an accident Papa-san had in early May while cultivating berries. He was adjusting the harness on our normally gentle horse, Dolly, and she kicked him, breaking several of his ribs. Papa-san managed to get back to the house and Mama- san immediately called our family doctor.

The doctor told Papa-san he could not do any outdoor work for several weeks. He could risk puncturing a lung. It was the worst time to receive such news—just as he was getting ready for the first harvest since returning home. Papa-san protested, saying he had to work. Yoneichi was in the Army in Europe and there was no one else available.

The doctor offered to place an emergency request with the local American Red Cross so Yoneichi could be released from his military duties right away. The doctor did not think this would be a problem because the war was over, and farming was an essential industry.

Yoneichi returned to the farm in mid-June 1946. He had to skip the victory parade in Washington, D.C., in July at which President Truman honored the 442nd Battalion. Yoneichi thought it was more important to be home in time to harvest the strawberries than to be honored as a hero. His devotion to our parents was primary.

Yoneichi was home for only a week when he took legal matters into his own hands. He went to Seattle to talk things over with the lawyer who drew up the initial contract with the deputy sheriff in early 1942. The lawyer and Yoneichi discussed their options. One strategy was to sue Deputy Sheriff Hopkins, if necessary, to force him to pay the money he owed my family and to show the records for those four years of activities on our farm.

About a month later, Yoneichi returned to Seattle for a second meeting with the lawyer. Yoneichi looked over the record book that Hopkins had handed over. It was a mess—disorganized and incomplete.

"Hopkins brought me $2,000 in cash," the lawyer offered. "He said he was having trouble making ends meet and this is all he could come up with. It isn't much. If you want, we can sue him and make him pay more."

Yoneichi considered this option for a long time, sitting thoughtfully. He figured the deputy sheriff probably owed our family many times that amount. Finally, he responded, "No, the money is not the issue, it is the principle. This has been a terrible time for our family, and Hopkins added to our misery. I just want him to think about the dishonest way he's conducted himself and take ownership of his behavior. That's what I care about."

The lawyer nodded. "OK, I'll write you a check for the $2,000 and we can close this case."

Later, Yoneichi would tell me he held up his hand and said to the lawyer, "No, I don't want it. No amount of money can make up for what our family went through. You helped us save our farm during a time when we really needed help. I'd like you to accept this money. Thank you very much. I appreciate all you have done for us."

The lawyer stared, dumbfounded. "You can't be serious," he said. "How will you pay your debts?"

Yoneichi answered calmly, "It's only money. In time, we will earn more. Money should be exchanged honestly and willingly with respect for both sides."

Yoneichi stood up, preparing to leave. "The important thing is that we still have our farm."

It was not until much later that I finally understood why Deputy Sheriff Hopkins did not uphold his agreement with us to care for our farm. In October 1942, when we were held at the Tule Lake Internment Camp, Hopkins had visited us. Hopkins met with Yoneichi and Papa-san with an offer he thought our family could not refuse. He asked if they would sell our property to him.

Yoneichi and Papa-san politely listened to his proposal, but firmly refused. Hopkins left empty-handed after a 500-mile journey. I now believe his initial intentions in managing our farm were honest, but he gave in to the temptation to profit from our desperate situation.

In addition, there were many reasons why Hopkins may have had difficulties. Pickers were in scarce supply during the war. He undoubtedly had many other responsibilities, including caring for other farms besides ours. Over time, I decided Hopkins was more overwhelmed and unqualified to do the job than dishonest, but that did not excuse him for not communicating with us.

◅◉►

I finished nurse's training in July 1947. As soon as I finished the final exam, I boarded a train for home. It had been two and a half years since I had seen my family. I could hardly wait to see them. When I got to Seattle, I hurried to the bus station, called home, and got on the next bus that commuted via the ferry to Vashon Island. The ride across Puget Sound was the same as before, only the ferry had traveled the local waters thousands of times in the five years I had been gone. The air was balmy and peaceful, and the blue summer sky as wide open as welcoming arms.

Once on the island, I looked closely at all the houses and yards, the trees, and the familiar stores in little downtown Vashon. I wanted to note everything that had changed and everything that had remained the same. As we approached our road, I stood up and walked to the front of the bus. There was the familiar Matsuda mailbox and straight dirt road that led to our home.

I almost ran down the road, gripping my **footlocker**. I arrived breathless and stood still for a moment looking at the farmhouse. Mama-san looked out of the kitchen window and immediately came out. We met in front of the porch and embraced. This was the second time we ever hugged, and we smiled.

After years away from our home, I heard my mother's wonderful, familiar greeting: *"Okaeri nasai."* (Welcome home.)

I responded, *"Tadaima kaerimashita."* (I have just returned home.) These were words I had waited five years to say.

I greeted Papa-san with the same words and with a slight bow, then a firm grip with my right hand. I hugged Yoneichi for a long time. I could hardly believe I was really home.

At last, we were all together again.

⊰◉⊱

Mama-san had prepared a delicious dinner of sushi and vegetables. As we all sat down together at the table, just as we had always done before, Yoneichi and I looked at Mama-san and said, *"Itadaki masu."* (I gratefully receive this meal you have prepared for us.)

Mama-san replied, *"Dozo. Itadaki masho."* (Let's eat!)

None of us could stop smiling as we talked about the relief of being together again at our own table in our home. We also talked about Mack and how well he took care of our farm while we were gone. After my parents returned to Vashon, Mack decided to move to California where it is warmer.

During the meal, I observed my parents and Yoneichi when they weren't looking to see how they might have changed since I had seen them last. My parents' hair was a little whiter and Papa-san's was a little thinner in front. They had more wrinkles but a healthier, leaner look from working the farm.

Yoneichi looked different. His youthful, carefree manner was gone. He talked less, looked at each of us and listened more intently. In addition to the new lines on his face, he looked more serious and stone-faced. His usual light-hearted bantering and joking were replaced by thoughtful glances and a slow nodding of his head. The war had aged and hardened my brother.

That first night home I was so relieved and joyful that Yoneichi was alive, I did not fully consider what the war might have done to him. Not until years later would I realize he was tested and shaped by his war experience in ways only other veterans could understand.

That night at the dinner table I realized that I had changed, too. I left five years earlier a frightened, confused, angry girl. Now, I had returned as an independent young woman with professional skills to make my own way in the world.

I had faced the trauma and contradictions of the evacuation and four internment camps. In time, I learned to rise above the shock and depression to become a stronger person. I studied and worked hard to achieve my goal of becoming a registered nurse.

Mary at twenty-two years old in 1947, standing near Mama-san's roses.

MARY MATSUDA GRUENEWALD COLLECTION

When Yoneichi was overseas, I had worked diligently to help my parents sort out and secure the legal documents they needed to return to the farm. Because I had lived independently from them while facing professional demands, I had developed my own sense of self and ensured my self-sufficiency. Throughout the entire process, my parents taught me how to make their strengths my own.

❧❀❧

After lingering over dinner, we went outdoors. I looked around for Frisky; he was not sitting in his usual place on the porch.

"Frisky wasn't here when we got home," Mama-san said, long-ingly. "Mack didn't know what happened to him. He suspects Frisky went off into the woods after we left and just died." He was an old dog when we left.

A big lump rose in my throat. "How sad! He died alone, maybe feeling like we had abandoned him." Frisky had been with us for so many years—ever since I was four years old. He was our loyal watchdog, and I was his loving friend throughout my childhood.

"I asked Mack about Kitty," Mama-san added. "He didn't know. She also disappeared sometime shortly after we left. She probably went out into the woods to look for food."

Mama-san and I walked along the eastern and southern bound-aries of our farm. I thought about how frightened we were on that fateful day five years earlier as we took this same walk.

Once again, we stood together and admired Mount Rainier off to the southeast, still looking majestic, streaked in the sunset's pink reflections. We lingered by Mama-san's vegetable garden. The dark green, feathery carrot tops waved gently in the breeze. Beanstalks were still producing pods, ready to be picked and enjoyed. Tender lettuce and beets would be ready to harvest in the next few weeks, and nearby strawberry plants looked healthy.

Fruit trees were loaded with maturing nectarines and apples. The pink and white carnations along the south and west sides of the house filled the night air with their perfume. All seemed right once again. Even the chickens clucking in the chicken yard, scratching for feed, sounded sweet.

While Mama-san and I walked back to the house, I thought, *Everything looks the same, and still wonderful. Only we have changed.*

CHAPTER TWENTY-SEVEN

MAMA-SAN

My parents and Yoneichi had many more happy years together on the farm.

Papa-san spent the rest of his life faithfully working the land with his son. Their roles changed, and Yoneichi became the head of the household. Although they always consulted each other regarding different decisions that had to be made, they both understood that Yoneichi was now in charge. That was the way things were done in the traditional Japanese family.

The farm work picked up until it ran as productively as it had before the War. Pickers came during the harvest and at 10:00 every morning, Papa-san handed out three pieces of candy to each picker for a break.

Every evening after dinner Papa-san sat in his big overstuffed chair in front of the oil stove, reading the newspaper until he fell asleep. Mama-san would awaken him for the evening snack, followed by a long, relaxing bath. After a good night's rest, the daily cycle would begin again. It was good to be home.

In 1952, the McCarran-Walter Act repealed the Oriental Exclusion Act, permitting first generation Japanese Americans, *Isseis*, like my parents to become naturalized citizens. In 1954, both of my parents studied for and successfully passed the exam to become citizens of the United States of America. It was the fulfillment of their lifelong dream. Even

MARY MATSUDA GRUENEWALD COLLECTION

Mama-san in the strawberry fields.

though it took them so many years, it gave them great satisfaction and a sense that all of their sacrifices had been worth it.

The career I began as a nurse's aide in Heart Mountain Relocation Camp led me to my life's work. I stayed at Vashon for only a few months in 1947 while I made future plans and reassured myself that everything was settled on the farm. Then I moved to Seattle and began my career as a registered nurse.

While attending the College of Puget Sound to work toward my bachelor's degree, I met my future husband, Charles E. Gruenewald.

We married in 1951, then moved to Boston, Massachusetts, where he completed his Master's Degree in Sacred Theology at Boston University School of Theology. During our time there, I worked for the Visiting Nurse Association.

After the completion of his studies, Charles and I returned to the West Coast where we served Methodist churches in Cosmopolis and Renton, Washington. We also lived and worked in Idaho Falls, Idaho, and Denver, Colorado.

In Denver, while Charles worked on a doctorate degree, I worked with a team of private-duty nurses caring for patients of three heart surgeons. It was an exciting time medically because open-heart surgery was a new medical procedure. The work was challenging, exciting, and occasionally tragic when we lost a patient.

As a minister's wife, I met many wonderful people and worked tirelessly to learn the many facets of that role. I also became a mother, bearing a daughter and two sons between 1954 and 1960.

⋋◎⋌

In the summer of 1965, my three young children and I visited the family farm on Vashon to help with the harvest, as we had every year. The harvest season was at its peak, and Papa-san and Yoneichi were in the strawberry fields daily with a host of pickers. Mama-san, 73, had been struggling with stomach cancer during the previous year, and we knew her time was running short.

Each morning I would awaken the children at 6:00, fix their breakfast, and take them to Mama-san's bedside. My oldest child, Martha, was eleven, and she was hesitant to get too close because Grandma looked quite thin and sickly. David was nine, and he looked at Grandma intently as he approached her bedside and stood close to her. Ray was only five, and he snuggled up to Grandma in spite of her appearance. They all knew something was wrong, although Ray was too young to understand what it meant.

Mama-san would smile at them, nod, and say to me in Japanese, "They are a little afraid of me because I look so thin and different, aren't they? That's all right. Work hard, little ones, and help your mother, your uncle, and grandpa, okay?"

I translated her message to them. When the children ran off to the fields to pick strawberries, I gave Mama-san medicine for her pain. Then I gave her tea or whatever she felt like eating. After she ate, I bathed her, took care of her personal needs, and helped her to settle comfortably for the next few hours.

One afternoon she opened the top drawer of her dresser. Silently, she picked up her gold wedding band from its box. She slipped it on her thin ring finger, looked at it for a moment, and then returned it to the box. She looked content as she slowly got back into bed.

The following morning she looked especially alert, bright, and radiant. "Wherever I look, I see God as a glowing, white light beckoning me down this long corridor to come to Him," explained Mama-san. "God has given me a good life, and I know I will be going to a more wonderful, beautiful place. I want to go as soon as I can."

This was the way Mama-san looked at each new experience. She was always ready to take the next step. Now, she was facing the end of her life with the same openness and faith that was so characteristic of her. At one point, I burst into tears, dropped to my knees beside her bed, put my head on her shoulder, and held her while I wept.

We stayed that way for some time until my crying eased. With one final attempt, I sat up and asked hopefully, "What would your answer be if a cure for cancer were to be found tomorrow? Would you be willing to stay?"

"No," she answered. "My work on earth is done. You and your brother are adults now. You both have families to care for, and it is time for me to leave."

She shifted her position in bed so she could face me directly. Mama-san paused and looked at me apologetically, then added,

"But there are some things I must discuss with you. I can't erase from my memory that time in camp when I know Papa-san and I pushed you so hard when you had so many other burdens."

Then she added, "And I am especially troubled by that time fourteen years ago when you asked for our blessing in marrying the *hakujin* (white man), Charles. I owe you my deepest apologies for my rejection of him. In looking back, I should have accepted your choice and been glad for you. Please forgive us for what we did."

I was astonished that she could think about those things when she was so close to death. I put my hand gently on her shoulder as I replied, "I understood. I never blamed you for either of those things. I know it was hard for you when I first told you about Charles, but look how things have worked out. Charles is such an important part of our family now. And all the hard work we had to do during that very difficult time has really paid off. We have our farm back. It was worth all the effort. No forgiveness is necessary."

Mama-san smiled with a look of satisfaction on her face. I smiled back and silently took her pale, thin hand in mine.

From that moment on, as often as her strength would allow, we spent the next five days together recalling memories about our years together. We talked about my childhood triumphs and traumas, long lost friends, and her hopes for my future. We recalled simple pleasures; a cool breeze on a hot day, the satisfaction of sharing ice cream bars with all of the pickers at the end of the harvest, and cooking meals together in the kitchen. A peace came over both of us.

I made it a point to check on Mama-san hourly. The morning of June 30, I checked at 8:00. She was sleeping comfortably from the pain medicine I had given her earlier. When I returned an hour later, Mama-san was lying motionless with a **blissful** look on her face. I held my breath as I crept closer. Her chest was no longer rising and falling.

In the stillness, I knelt by her side, placed my hands on her hands, bowed my head and wept. I did not want to let her go. Mama-san was my strength, my inspiration, and my anchor. It did not make her departure any easier knowing that she had faith and courage in facing her final transition.

When I thought I had no more tears to shed, I got up and gathered a basin of warm water, clean towels, a fresh bar of Ivory soap and a bottle of Jergen's Lotion. Carefully, I bathed and dried Mama-san's face, ears, and neck. I thought about how often she must have bathed me when I was young. Then I gently bathed her body, thin and ravaged by cancer. My mother was always a petite woman but now she had become a mere shadow of her former weight. Her skin looked fragile and translucent.

I thought about all the other bodies I had bathed as a nurse, but it was nothing like bathing Mama-san's. Hers was the source of my life, the one that nourished me physically, mentally, and emotionally. My tears flowed as I washed her one last time.

Carefully, I rubbed the lotion on Mama-san's skin, then dressed her in a clean nightgown. I combed her long gray hair, straightened the covers on her bed, and placed her hands in prayer on her chest.

Then I went out to the field to get Papa-san and Yoneichi. I approached them and without a word, they each knew what had happened. They came to the house with stricken faces.

Papa-san looked briefly at her and, to my surprise, said, "She's just asleep." He promptly left the room.

Yoneichi came into the bedroom, dropped down beside her, put his arm across her body and wept. I stood beside him and wept as well. We stayed that way for a long time.

Even though nothing had been said, word passed quickly among the pickers who were at the farm that day. Mama-san's illness was common knowledge and several people knew instantly what it meant when I summoned my father and brother. Many of the workers who knew Mama-san shed tears in the strawberry fields that day.

I called our doctor, and he notified the **mortician**, who arrived within the hour to pick up Mama-san's body. Soon the house was a hubbub of activity as the day's work ended and people began arriving in droves. I was only vaguely aware of the many people who came and went, expressing their sympathy and offering support.

My three children picked strawberries all day long and were unaware of their Grandma's passing. When they came back to the house they were bewildered by all the activity. Then they saw the empty bed where Grandma normally slept. The two oldest children took it upon themselves to comfort the youngest and explain what happened.

The next day, the harvest continued as usual. Because Mama-san's death occurred during the height of the picking season, we requested that her remains be cremated and the ashes placed in the gravesite we had selected for her. We scheduled her memorial service for later in the summer, as she would have wished. Mama-san was a very sensible woman.

≺◉≻

Papa-san eventually came to accept his wife's death, but he did so in the privacy of his own thoughts. I never saw him cry for her, but he did spend a great deal of time alone, working the fields.

One day, about two months after her death, I began talking about Mama-san in front of my father. He remarked with obvious pride that she had come from a long line of samurai. After that, something opened up inside Papa-san and he was able to talk about many memories with his wife. That was when I knew Papa-san had made his peace with her death.

In the weeks that followed, especially in the evenings after the children were asleep, I wandered around the yard that Mama-san loved so much. I looked to the stars for some kind of answer to where she was.

Earlier in the year, when Mama-san was still well enough to venture outdoors, she planted peas knowing full well she would not be here to eat them. She started tomatoes she would never see ripen, and planted cuttings of chrysanthemums knowing that others would enjoy their beauty.

Over the years, I would come to know Mama-san's wisdom and grace that would continue to flourish and bloom in my life in unexpected and mysterious ways.

≈⊚≈

Just before our family was broken up at Heart Mountain in 1944, with each of us going in different directions, Mama-san offered a great piece of wisdom. She suggested that we imagine what it would be like twenty years in the future to look back on our experiences in the internment camps.

As it turned out, her death occurred twenty years after that wise suggestion—and it was just as we had imagined. She helped us build a map for the future and allowed us to hope at a time when others might have despaired.

The stories I told my own children and grandchildren were not Japanese fairy tales about Momotaro. Instead, I told them about the real-life bravery of their uncle Yoneichi, the calm strength of Papa-san, and especially the wisdom, courage, and grace of Mama-san.

It was her voice I heard during difficult times. It was Mama-san's smile I would remember when an unexpected joy caught my attention and made me smile. And it was her strength that I would continue to carry with me every day, even while writing my memoir almost forty years after her death.

While the internment experience was a tragedy, because of Mama-san I am at peace with it. And I am even grateful that I lived through it.

RETURN TO MINIDOKA INTERNMENT CAMP

In the summer of 2004, I returned to Minidoka, sixty years after I had left. I joined 130 *Isseis*, *Niseis* and *Sanseis* (third generation Japanese Americans) nationwide to attend a special pilgrimage by former internees and their families to the internment camp. Earlier, I had participated in meetings along with other Japanese Americans and National Park Superintendent Neil King and his staff, who were preparing to create a new National Monument memorializing the Minidoka Internment Camp.

When we reached Minidoka after a twelve-hour bus ride from Seattle, I was eager to see what the National Park Service had created. At the first stop, I was surprised to find only a single barrack standing alone, with no gate or guard towers nearby. Most of the original buildings had been sold or moved away for use as storage buildings. However, I knew that later we would go to another site where we would see what remained of the original camp entrance.

When I stepped onto the porch of a typical barrack and walked through the doorway of the end apartment, I was suddenly back in 1944. I put my hand to my throat and took a deep breath trying to relax the tightness in my chest. The wide gaps between the planks in the floor brought back memories of the frequent windstorms that whipped up dust through every crack and space in the floorboards, walls, and window frames. Automatically, I closed my eyes as if to avoid the sting of the dirt and sand on my face and in my mouth.

On that calm summer day in 2004, I once again felt suffocated and **claustrophobic**. As if it were only yesterday, I still hated this place where I was held against my will.

Once again, shame constricted my throat after all these years and I had trouble speaking to the people around me. Other Japanese Americans, many of them third generation (*Sansei*) and fourth generation (*Yonsei*), wanted to learn about the evacuation and the imprisonment. They wanted to connect with those of us who lived in the internment camps and hear our experiences.

Nearing my eightieth year, I knew I needed to tell them what it was like for me, but I was reluctant to speak—just as I had been for so many years.

I could not bring myself to speak.

Later in the day, we went on a mile-long tour led by a guide. We walked through tall grass looking at the places where the National Park Service had started to recreate and label a small part of the original camp. We looked at what used to be the entryway adjacent to the military police building with its standing stone wall and a fireplace. This had been a heavily guarded area, one that no one could enter or leave without clearance from the military police. Now, I walked freely. I wanted to fling my arms into the air and shout "Freedom!" but I kept a reserved presence.

Just inside the entrance I saw a terrible blank space. Once, this public entryway had displayed a large wooden sign made and erected by internees, listing the names of the men from Minidoka Internment Camp who served in the U.S. Army during World War II. My brother's name would not have appeared there, since he had departed for the war from Heart Mountain Internment Camp.

Minidoka's Honor Roll had stood beside a Japanese-style garden made by an internee skilled in creating beautiful Japanese gardens. The Honor Roll was gone and no one seemed to know when or why it was removed, or by whom. I clenched my jaws. To remove this symbol of the ultimate sacrifice of our young men at a time of such hardship was unthinkable to me. I wanted to believe someone had carefully removed it and preserved it in some safe place for later recognition and honor. But I couldn't speak up and ask.

Still in a daze, I accompanied the others as we continued the tour to look at the original root cellar, which had been used to store root vegetables for the camp. Then we paused at the old swimming hole, now mostly hidden by a dense growth of trees and grass.

Yes, I thought to myself, *life went on for us in the camps.*

The following day we returned to the Minidoka National Monument site for a memorial service with flags and a *Nisei* veterans honor guard. I thought of the mothers of these soldiers, like Mama-san, who showed remarkable courage and sacrifice during those war years. Just like many other American parents, Mama-san and Papa-san had sent their only son off to risk his life in the fight for his homeland. But most parents didn't make that courageous decision from behind barbed wire.

~◎~

During lunch, I sat with two women from Japan and another *Nisei* woman. In our conversation I mentioned that I had never visited Japan. This resulted in startled looks, protests, and questions from the others. I explained that some years ago a *Nisei* friend had taken a group of doctors to Japan. Because he looked like a Japanese citizen, he said he was publicly ridiculed because he did not speak the language "properly."

"I have never forgotten that," I said. "I am not willing to put myself into that position."

The ladies protested that Japan isn't like that anymore. The attitudes had changed over the last twenty years. They reassured me that there are signs with English wording, and many Japanese understand English. They said I was missing out on an important life experience.

I had never explored the reasons for my reluctance to visit my parents' homeland. Later, I realized that it was one thing to be wounded by the rejection of American society during and after World War II. However, I was haunted by the prospect that I could be rejected yet again—this time by the Japanese society of my ancestors.

The evacuation came at a time when I was struggling with my identity. The pressure to appear "loyal" to the United States caused me to bury my "Japanese self" for decades. This lunchtime discussion inspired me to begin changing my thinking and explore more of my life, especially the part of me that is Japanese.

It took me sixty years to come to terms with who I am. The country of my ancestors is no longer my enemy. Now, I was ready to reconsider a visit to Japan.

~☉~

The next day we headed back to Seattle. While on the bus, one of the coordinators extended an invitation to the *Niseis* to share their experiences of internment camps. I thought, *Maybe I should try again to speak up in spite of how hard it might be.*

Once again, my chest tightened, and my heart quickened. I had been saddled by feelings of paralyzing helplessness for so long. This time, instead of using my own words, I decided to read my mother's letters that I had brought with me. I thought, *Maybe Mama-san, always eloquent, could reach across the seeming generation gap.* I stood up and weaved my way to the front of the bus as it sped down the highway. I clutched the letters to my chest.

Sitting down in one of the front aisle seats, I turned to face the back of the bus and selected the first letter. Taking the microphone

in my left hand, I looked up and saw all of the Japanese faces looking at me expectantly. Then I pictured Mama-san's smiling face,
calm and steady, and this gave me strength.

"My brother had left for the army," I began, "and I was taking
classes in the U.S. Cadet Nurse Corps program in Clinton, Iowa.
My mother left Minidoka Internment Camp for Ogden, Utah to
work in a vegetable-canning factory. She wrote this letter to me
shortly after leaving for Utah."

September 3, 1944
    Mary-san, I arrived in Ogden at 3:30. Please be
relieved. After many, many miles of sagebrush, we finally
arrived in Ogden. From the beginning to the end of our
journey, it was sagebrush. It's beyond talking about—all
this sagebrush along straight roads. It felt wonderful.
    I wish we could have been together, you and I. The
image of your face in the bus window [when I had left
her] remains with me. Please be sure and take care of
your body.
    Mama

I looked outside and saw the same sagebrush my mother
described as she left Minidoka for the first time. Then I pulled out
the next letter and began to read:

March 6, 1945
    Mary-san, I am sorry for delaying so long to send you
this letter, but I suspect you remain energetic and dis-
charging your duty. Letters do not come from Yoneichi-
san. It is really, really lonely. And you are so far away.
    Every day I think about you and Yoneichi-san. No
matter how much I think about it or feel about it, and
know that it is shikata ga nai, I can't keep from thinking about it. I think he has gone overseas. I had a very
clear dream about him. Letters don't come to you from
him either, do they?
    Mama

I explained to the bus crowd, "I knew that my parents had sent their only son into battle knowing that he might die. That was the common philosophy among all Japanese."

As I read Mama-san's letters, all written in Japanese, I suddenly became aware that my voice sounded like hers. I paused where she would have paused. I emphasized the words she would have. Even when I translated the letters into English, it felt as though she was present. It was Mama-san's voice speaking to the third and fourth generations of Japanese Americans who were listening. Together, we were telling the next two generations our story.

Taking a deep breath, I composed myself and continued. "The final letter I'm going to read was written after my mother heard about the dropping of the atom bombs on Japan. Most of you know our parents were not allowed to become citizens of the United States for many years, so they were still citizens of Japan. My parents had chosen to come to America to live, and remained faithful to their dream, in spite of the betrayal of the principles of liberty for them. They never imagined that the war would end this way."

Then I read Mama-san's letter dated August 17, 1945.

Mary-san, Japan is a small country. But from a long time ago, she has never lost a single war. In order to beat Japan, America took the sky for its own side and tried to crush small Japan.

They took this bad bomb and they tried to obliterate Japan. The residue that remains in the history of the universe is a great shame/disgrace. We are not talking about it; we may want to hide from it, but we can't hide from it.

This wonderful America should not have done this. We cannot forget what has happened.

Mama

メリーさん あなたの氣持は よく
わかりました ありがとう
「日本は小さい國では それでも
むかしから ぺんも まけた こと
はないのですね その日本をまか
すのに アメリカは せかいをじぶ
のさしどに ひきよせて 小さい日本
をつぶそうとしている のです
こんと 日本へ おとした バクダンは
あれは せかいで つかぶ ことのでき
ない、バードな バクダンを もって日本
をなくしよー とするのです
これは アメリカをして せかいのレキシ
にのこる 大きな ハジ であります
今のうちは ママたち なにも はな
しません けれども これは かくそう
としても かくす ことの できない
ことです りっぱな アメリカ として する
ことでは ないのです ほかの人には
ことでは なくても よろしい から アメリカ
はなさ なくても こんな ことを した
でも こんな ことを した ことを わすれ
ては なりません」

Mama-san's letter commenting on the atomic bomb.

I looked down at the sea of mostly Japanese faces, everyone's eyes watched me closely. No one moved or said a thing. My hands trembled as I tried to focus on the letter. We all knew I said publicly what many Japanese Americans had kept to themselves. In 1945, none of us dared to criticize America for dropping the atom bombs.

After a few moments, I stood to return to my seat in the rear of the bus. Two women sitting on either side of the bus near the front, gray-haired *Niseis* like me, stood up, put their hands out to touch me and thank me. They both had faraway looks on their faces.

My mother's words—more powerful than mine—had reached across the divide.

AFTERWORD

Several decades later, Japanese Americans fought for, and finally received, a formal apology from the United States government for wrongfully imprisoning Japanese Americans during World War II. The government acknowledged that "a grave injustice was done to both citizens and permanent residents of Japanese ancestry by the evacuation, relocation, and internment of civilians during World War II." The U.S. Constitution's First Amendment guarantees its citizens the right to petition the government for a "**redress of grievances**," which basically means to make right what was wrong.

President Ronald Reagan signed the Civil Liberties Act of 1988 into law on August 10 of that same year. This legislation acknowledged that the internment of Japanese Americans was based on "race prejudice, war hysteria, and a failure of political leadership." Each surviving internee received a letter of apology from the President and a one-time payment of $20,000. The Government also provided funds for public education on the internment so future generations of Americans would learn about the internment of Japanese Americans during World War II.

The Civil Liberties Act was a triumph of more than a decade of effort by many Japanese-American activists nationwide. U.S. Senator Daniel Inouye from Hawaii was a *Nisei* and a decorated veteran of the 442nd Regimental Combat Team. He recommended that the U.S. government establish the Commission on Wartime Relocation and Internment of Civilians in order to hold fact-finding hearings across the country.

From July to December 1981, hundreds of Japanese Americans testified before the Commission and the national press. Often for the first time, they told their stories of imprisonment in internment camps that had taken place thirty-five years earlier. Their heart-wrenching stories moved and shocked the nation, helping to change public opinion in support of the movement to correct this injustice.

In many cases, this process also opened a dialog with third- and fourth- generation Japanese Americans. Many families never talked about what happened to Japanese Americans during World War II. So, their children were unaware of what their own parents and grandparents had lived through.

The U.S. government's process of correcting a wrong through the redress of grievances brought healing and a sense of legiti-macy to the Japanese Americans' experiences. When I received my formal apology dated October 3, 1990 and signed by President George H. W. Bush, I felt a sense of satisfaction. I also felt regret that my parents and my brother did not live to see the resolution of this terrible wrong.

The National Japanese American Memorial to Patriotism in Washington, D.C., was built in honor all of those who were interned and the *Nisei* soldiers who died during World War II. I attended the dedication in November 2000, along with a crowd of my peers—all of us with gray hair and wrinkles. We had held back so many emotions for 58 years. At the dedication, many of us cried silently—alone, and with each other.

As I looked up at the 14-foot bronze sculpture of two cranes—symbolizing happiness, good fortune, and longevity—enmeshed in barbed wire, I was overwhelmed with contradictory feelings. Joy for the long-sought recognition of our suffering, and sadness for those who died and never saw this day of celebration. I wept for my family and for all peoples of all times who have suffered oppression and hopelessness in the face of overwhelming odds.

My parents would have wept, just as I did, but they would have felt a great deal of pride in the accomplishments of our people and would have known that they had contributed to the memorial's completion. But they would have been even more proud if they knew about an honor that was bestowed upon me less than two years later.

The career I began as a nurse's aide in an internment camp would culminate in my being invited to the White House along with other health reform lobbyists to speak with the President. For most of my career as a registered nurse I had worked at Group Health Cooperative, a health-care organization in Seattle, Washington.

The Japanese Crane Monument is a bronze sculpture created by Nina Akamu.

While in Washington, D.C. , I returned to the National Japanese American Memorial site with two Caucasian companions. Once again, I was overcome by memories of those difficult times. Sixty years later and the tears still flowed. My friends silently put their arms around me.

Again, I read the names of the *Nisei* men who had died in battle for our freedom and dignity. They had gone ahead courageously and paved the way for the rest of us. In front of the reflecting pool, I pondered what Mama-san would think about this memorial. I could see her nodding and smiling, making the point that every-thing had worked out all right. We had all demonstrated *gaman* (patience) and the difficult times had passed.

The next day, I joined my colleagues at the White House and I briefly met and spoke with President George W. Bush in a carefully organized ceremony. I spoke for the health care reform legislation and urged swift action. Afterward, I attended a press conference with the President, satisfied with my participation and over-whelmed with the spectacle surrounding the event.

That evening in my hotel room, when I was alone writing down my thoughts, I came to a stunning realization: *My return to the Memorial occurred exactly 60 years to the day after the evacuation from our Vashon home on May 16, 1942—and the very next day I met with the President of the United States of America.*

This realization swept over me. *How could it be that I would be in this place at this time?* I wondered.

I didn't try to figure it out. I just bowed my head in thanksgiv-ing for the mysteries of life—the mystery that brought me to such a place of fulfillment and completion sixty years later to the day.

Mama-san was right. In my greatest moments of despair in the internment camps, she had asked, *"What kind of memories will we want to have in twenty years of how we faced these difficulties now?"*

⊰❀⊱

Sixty years after the war, our strawberry farm is still in the fam-ily name, although its purpose has changed. The rows of straw-berries have been replaced by fields of grass that are occasionally mowed for hay.

My brother's wife still lives in our family home. The pond on which Yoneichi and I used to glide on our makeshift raft is still there with frogs that croak on warm summer evenings. Madrona trees still grow to the west of our property, but most of the ever-green trees are gone, logged and removed.

Mama-san's carnations on the south side of the house are gone, but her Silver Pine tree has grown tall and stately. Snowcapped Mount Rainier, ever constant as human history unfolds, is still spiritually stirring.

Papa-san lived out the rest of his days missing Mama-san but content, living in the home that he built and passed on to his son. After many years working the land, Papa-san eventually became forgetful. At times, he wandered off and a kind neighbor would bring him home. He peacefully slipped away in his sleep one night at the age of 93.

After World War II, Yoneichi earned enough money to buy more land and equipment, eventually owning and farming 52 acres. In

Yoneichi and Marjorie Matsuda in December 1968 with their four daughters; Marlene, 8, and Kathryn, 5, (front), Marguerite, 2, (in her dad's arms), and Sheila, 1.

1958, he married Marjorie Nakagawa and reared a family of four daughters. Tragically, Marjorie died from cancer in 1973. Four years later, Yoneichi married Miyoko Nishi. To this day, my sister-in-law Miyoko and I are close, sharing many traveling adventures together.

Yoneichi taught social studies and the Japanese language for eighteen years at Ingraham High School in Seattle. He hoped the next generation would see the world through wiser eyes. After a full day of teaching classes, he would take the ferry home to Vashon and prepare for the next day's classes. Then he cultivated the strawberries in the dark, riding his tractor with the lights on.

Yoneichi decided to retire early because he had heard teachers don't live very long after retirement. He wanted to travel and had already made plans for an extended trip to Japan with his wife and daughters. One evening, less than three months after his retirement in 1985, Yoneichi was on his tractor cultivating strawberries when he had the first signs of a heart attack.

He was rushed to the hospital, and despite receiving superb medical care, his condition deteriorated. A week later, he died surrounded by family.

After Yoneichi's death, I wandered through my days lost, unable to believe that he could really be gone. I felt cheated, anguished, and horribly disappointed that we never had our lengthy conversations about his war experiences. It would be years later while writing this book that I pieced together some sense of Yoneichi's war experience through my readings and by interviewing his war buddies.

I still visit Vashon and walk the family farm. Just down the road from our home is the Vashon Island Cemetery where my parents and brother are buried. Yoneichi had been one of the commissioners of the King County Cemetery District No. 1 for nine years. At the entrance to the cemetery, the county established a beautiful memorial garden for Yoneichi. Whenever I visit the cemetery, I pause at the memorial garden, gaze at the plaque and the garden's array of flowers. I have never stopped longing for my courageous brother who always worked to guide and support me, as he did others.

In time, I realized I would have to carry forward the family's courage. Telling my story would be my way.

Not until the 1990s did some *Niseis* begin to talk openly about their internment experiences, and yet even today, many of my contemporaries are still reluctant to discuss this time in U.S. history. Some *Sanseis*, the children of the *Niseis* who went through the internment, have asked, "Why didn't you fight back?" or "Why did you go like sheep to be slaughtered without any resistance?"

Their questions made me rethink my experience and helped me realize the need to tell my story.

In my seventies, I began to write down my story, reliving it all once again. Now in my eighties, I often tell the world my story of imprisonment. In these tumultuous, post 9/11 times, it is crucial that I tell my story. Perhaps if I share my experiences, this will

Mary with her three children, Ray (standing), David, and Martha.

be one more convincing piece of evidence against the possibility of internment camps in the United States ever happening again.

⊶◎⊷

New Year's Day 2005, my three grown children and my grandson were looking at the three jars of shells Mama-san and I had collected at Tule Lake more than sixty years ago. The old glass jars seem fragile with their slightly rusted, screw-on lids of different sizes. One has a faded, torn label that says "Dill Pickles." Each of the jars holds a different kind of shell.

I keep these jars in a cabinet in my basement. Every so often I take them out. I run my fingers along the rough edges of the spiral shells and luminous white clamshells. Some are broken, yet still precious in detail.

I scoop up handfuls of these delicate reminders of a bittersweet time. *Mama-san touched these shells too,* I say to myself as I recall the simple pleasure of working side-by-side with her collecting these shells that seemed to transport us far beyond that painful time in our history.

Many years later my son, Ray, counted all the shells in the three glass jars. Unknowingly, Mama-san and I had collected about 120,000 shells—one for every man, woman, and child who was interned during the War.

As my children and I talk about the seashells and Mama-san, I hear her soft voice and see her face as she nods and smiles at us. While I received priceless gifts of wisdom and love from my parents, I have nothing tangible of theirs from the old country. What few treasures they brought from Japan were burned that evening in 1942 in a desperate attempt to avoid being identified with the enemy.

Now, these shells have become my family's new cultural treasures to pass on to future generations, along with my story. 🦐

ACKNOWLEDGMENTS

I want to thank the many people who helped to make this book possible. First and foremost are the members of my original family: my mother, father and brother, all of whom died long ago, but whose memory remains vivid and central to this story. My children, Martha, David and Ray, and my nieces, Marlene, Kathryn, Marguerite and Sheila, were my primary inspiration for writing my story late in life. My sister-in-law, Miyoko, supported me and gave me specific mementos from my brother's collection of books and papers.

I want to remember Tok Otsuka and Augie Takatsuka, who served in the 100th/442nd Regimental Combat Team with my brother. From them, I learned about the battles they fought for the Allied forces and for the freedom of our people. I also wish to remember Tok's sister, Haru Ishikawa, a trusted friend who helped confirm the truth of my experience of the internment. She was like the sister I never had.

My writing teacher Brenda Peterson played a significant role in the writing of this story as did the students in the writing class. They included Leigh Calvez, Claire Dederer, Liz Gruenfeld, Leslie D. Helm, Susan Little, J. Kingston Pierce, Trip Quillman, John Runyan, Dori Jones Yang, Denise Benitez, Jordan Buck, Kristina Danilchik, Cathy Englehart, Laurie Greig, Anne Hayden, Donna Kelleher, Susan Knox, Tara Kolden, Anne Mize, Trish Murphy, Ginny NiCarthy, Kimberly Richardson, Ward Serill, Julie Stonefelt, and Louise Wisechild.

I am deeply grateful for the support of Robert S. Fisher of the Wing Luke Museum and Carolyn Marr of the Museum of History and Industry. They made it both possible and pleasant for me to include valuable photographs from their collections.

I wish to give special thanks to my son, Ray, who gave his heart, soul, expertise and energy to this book. His contributions helped me to write my story and complete this project that was so important to me. While his time and efforts were indispensable, it was his interest, passion and support that meant so much to me. I can think of no greater gift that he could have given our whole family and me.

I would also like to acknowledge NewSage Press' book designer, Sherry Wachter, for her exquisite design sensibilities, which helped bring my story to life on these pages.

And finally, my profound thanks must go to Maureen R. Michelson, publisher of NewSage Press, for the extraordinary editing and personal support she provided. She recognized the potential in my story and helped to transform my initial manuscript into a polished work. It was her suggestion to create a young readers' edition of this book.

AUTHOR INTERVIEW

Q: *When did you decide to write a book about your experiences in Japanese-American internment camps? What inspired you to start writing?*

A: I began my initial writing efforts in 1995 after my son David asked about what happened to our family during World War II. When my children were young, I had told them little stories about the internment camps, in particular the lighter side of life at that time. I never spoke about the difficult experiences. In 1999, Seattle writer and teacher, Brenda Peterson, invited me to join her writing class, and I realized I was ready to begin writing seriously about my experiences. At first, I thought I was just writing down my story to share with my family. But after a few years, around 2002, my writing teacher and classmates strongly encouraged me to consider writing a book for publication.

Mary Matsuda Gruenewald

GROUP HEALTH COOPERATIVE

Q: *How long did it take you to write your book and what was that experience like?*

A: It took me about 10 years to get the story out of me and onto the paper. So, I began writing when I was 70 years old, and held my first published book in my hands when I turned 80 years old!

Initially, I was frustrated and discouraged because I had buried my feelings about all those years in the internment camps. I had to overcome the Japanese cultural norm of keeping silent about one's painful experiences. Traditionally, Japanese people do not openly express or discuss their disappointments or struggles. Also, when I began writing, I didn't want to show my grown children how I felt about being imprisoned in internments camps. I was afraid I would begin to cry and not be able to stop.

Once I got over my fear of opening up, I did spend a lot of time crying, mostly when I was alone sitting in front of my computer. I had to remember the pain wrapped up in all those memories in order to be able to write about them. My writing teacher and my seven classmates were very supportive during this process.

One of the assignments my writing teacher gave me to help me overcome my resistance to opening up was to buy a Japanese doll to replace the ones my family burned prior to our evacuation. Another thing that helped me open up to the memories and my deep feelings was to buy a CD with a Japanese song, *"Sakura,"* that was so familiar to me during my childhood. Sakura means cherry blossom in Japanese. It is a simple, beautiful melody that helped me to reconnect with what it is like to be Japanese.

Q: What was it like to remember the events from your youth and write about them?

A: It was extremely difficult to go back and explore and feel the emotions that accompanied our evacuation more than 50 years earlier. Once I began writing, it was like the dam broke: the emotions gushed out of me at times so intensely that I had to stop whatever I was doing and allow myself to feel the pain, fear, disappointment and anger before I could continue.

Q: *Did you learn new things while you researched and wrote your book?*

A: Yes, many things. I didn't know much about the courage of the soldiers of the 442nd Regimental Combat Team, who fought so bravely in Europe during World War II. Since my brother, Yoneichi, never spoke about the War, I had to turn to books to find out what he went through as a soldier. In fact, I didn't even know my brother was awarded a Bronze Star for bravery until after he died many years after the War.

I also learned much more about the difficulties within the Japanese-American community regarding the Loyalty Oath we all had to sign while in the internment camps. At the time I was 18 years old and I only understood the "Yes Yes" side of the argument. More than 50 years later while researching for my book, my eyes were opened to understanding the other side of the argument—the families who signed "No No" to the Loyalty Oath. I didn't really understand Japanese-American families who disagreed with the U.S. government until I met and became close friends with a "No No" family, and heard their viewpoints.

In my research, I was especially glad to learn more about the movement that eventually lead to a formal apology from the President to all Japanese Americans held in internment camps, along with reparation payments to the survivors of the internment. This led me to study South Africa's Truth and Reconciliation Commission, established by President Nelson Mandela in 1995 to reveal the South African government's past racial injustices and resolve the conflicts in order to find national unity. In learning about Nelson Mandela, I found even more reasons why it is so important to look for ways to reduce conflict and work for reconciliation.

Q: Now that you are in your 80s, do the experiences in the intern-ment camps still affect you?

A: I have come to look at conflict in different ways. I am more at peace with myself, and more resolved to extend my efforts towards the needs of others.

Q: What did your children think when they read your memoir?

A: My children originally felt "exposed" when they read parts of my writing, but they were pleased to know how our family dealt with the difficulties during that time. They became even more proud of our family and learned a great deal of our family history that they didn't know before.

Q: Why did you decide to do a Young Reader's edition of your memoir?

A: I have always enjoyed speaking to young children and mid-dle-schoolers about my experiences in the Japanese-American internment camps, especially because I was only 17 when my family was removed from our home. In addition, I believe it is so important for children to understand all the parts of our country's history, even the parts we are not proud of. We can learn from our mistakes, and hopefully, not make those mistakes again.

My publisher and editor, Maureen R. Michelson, encouraged me to consider a Young Reader's edition of my memoir. I immediately recognized the importance of young people being exposed to the experiences of other young people who suffer judgment, rejection, and negative encounters based on outward appearances.

Q: How has writing this book changed your life?

A: As a published author, I am more in the public eye and find greater demands on my time. *Looking Like the Enemy* is a very personal story, and many readers are interested in sharing their own family's experiences with me. I have been touched by their stories and I have met many wonderful people as a result of writing my memoir.

I find it fascinating how some people are drawn to me because of this book. I think this is because no matter what happened to us, my family found the strength to overcome many obstacles and emerge even stronger as a result. My hope is readers will draw on the power of the written word in order to overcome their own difficulties.

I have heard many stories as fascinating as my own, and I often encourage people to write down their stories for their own families. Writing is a powerful way to heal, to connect, and to demonstrate love for other people. I would like nothing better than for some of my young readers to find out more about the stories of their own families, which are just as unique and important as my family's history is.

Q: Have you visited Japan? How did the Japanese people receive your story and your book?

A: I traveled on a three-week book tour throughout Japan in April, 2005. I found the people very gracious, accepting, and curious about the Japanese-American experience during World War II. Japan is an amazing country, and I was treated like royalty during my visit. It was a privilege and an honor to be welcomed there.

Q: How did your trip to Japan affect you? What was the most inspirational? What was the most difficult?

A: Before the trip, I was somewhat fearful about going since I had not spoken any Japanese since my mother died in 1965. I need not have worried. People were very gracious and helpful. I gave several book readings and shared my story with people in Japan.

The son of one of my cousins (on my mother's side) met me in Kyoto, Japan and he took me to meet his mother. She was the wife of my cousin who had died. Normally, gatherings in Japan are conducted in restaurants or other public places. I knew that it was a great honor to be invited into this 83 year-old woman's house to meet her. When I met Shizuko-san, the traditional Japanese form of greeting someone for the first time flowed spontaneously out of my mouth! It felt like my mother was inside of me addressing Shizuko-san in the formal, gracious way that was traditional in 1920. I was astonished and so was she. This was the first time I had spoken Japanese in 45 years!

I went to many other places in Japan and met many other wonderful people, but the highlight of the whole trip was meeting this relative.

Q: *What do you hope young people will get from reading your book?*

A: The title of the book says it in a nutshell. We should not judge people by the way they look.

Q: *As your book goes to press in 2010, what are you working on?*

A: I am working on a new book based upon the wisdom of my mother, which is now a part of who I am as an elder. I plan to have the book also available as an audio book and I will be the reader.

Q: *Do you have any final thoughts you'd like to share with your young readers?*

A: All of us are very much like one another regardless of our backgrounds or where we live in the world. We all need adequate food and shelter, as well as friendship and companionship. All of us need to be safe from harm of whatever kind and most of all, we need to be accepted for who we are, not for what we look like.

GLOSSARY OF
VOCABULARY WORDS

The following definitions apply specifically to words used in this book. Additional definitions may apply to these words, but they are not all listed here.

allegiance	the loyalty of a citizen to his or her government
assimilate	to adapt, to conform with the customs and attitudes of a group or nation
banish	to cast out or expel someone from a place or a country
bespectacled	wearing eyeglasses
birthright	a right or privilege a person has because of where he or she was born
blissful	extreme happiness
classified	a secret or information available to only certain people or governments
claustrophobic	uncomfortable in small places or crowded areas
communicable disease	an illness or disease that one person can catch from another person
conspirator	a person who plots to betray a group or government, a traitor
contaminant	something that pollutes or poisons
corsage	a small bunch of flowers worn at the shoulder or waist or on the wrist

counter-intelligence the activity of an organization to get information about the enemy to stop them, or to commit sabotage

discrimination the act of treating people differently based on how they look or what group they belong to

Downs Syndrome a human genetic disorder where babies are born with mild to severe mental retardation

footlocker a small trunk that usually contains a soldier's personal belongings

foreshadow to show or indicate something before it happens, a prediction

friendly fire in war when soldiers get hurt or killed by other soldiers fighting on the same side

gas rationing during the war the government controlled how much gasoline people could get because it was a scarce resource

grafting to insert a bud or shoot from one plant into a slit in the stem of another plant in which it continues to grow

hosiery stockings or socks

hymnal a book of hymns or songs for church

infamy shame or disgrace

internee a prisoner, or a person held against his or her will

jitterbug a fast moving, acrobatic dance with twirls, splits and somersaults

linguist a person who is skilled in several languages

mannequin a model of the human figure used to display clothes

martial law   temporary rule by military forces imposed on civilians, especially during war

mortician   a person who owns or operates a funeral home to prepare the dead for burial

naturalized citizen a person from another country who is granted citizenship in the United States

nausea   feeling sick in the stomach, also a sense of disgust

petition   a formal request, often to a group in authority or to a government

propaganda   information or rumors spread widely to harm or help a person, group, or nation

redress of grievances   a concept rooted in the First Amendment of the Constitution, allows citizens to petition the government to correct or compensate for a wrongdoing against its citizens

rescind   to repeal or withdraw

sabotage   to obstruct or destroy a cause, a plan, or physical object, often during time of war

sanitarium   a nursing home or institution for treating people with a chronic illness

shivaree   a noisy celebration with kettles, pans, and other noisemakers

stockade   a prison for people in the military

stoic   self-controlled, unemotional

stool pigeon   a slang word for an informer or someone who is a spy for the authorities

subordinate   a person placed in a lower order or rank, dependent

taboo   something that is prohibited or banned

talisman   an object that has markings that give the person wearing it special protection or powers

ticking   a strong cotton fabric

tuberculosis   an infectious disease that can affect different tissues in the body, especially the lungs

zealot   a person who is a fanatic or extreme activist

zoot suit   a popular man's suit in the early 1940s with baggy pants, a big jacket with wide lapels, and often worn with suspenders and a long watch chain

GLOSSARY OF JAPANESE WORDS AND PHRASES

The following Japanese words and phrases are used in this book. The English translations are given in the book's text, but are also included here for you to study separately.

Arigato	thank you, appreciate
Dozo	please, by all means
Enryo	restraint, modesty, humility
Gaman	patience, perseverance, self-restraint
Genki	in high spirits, vigorous
Geta	Japanese wooden clogs
Giri	a sense of duty, obligation and loyalty to family or group
Go	a Japanese board game
Gochiso sama deshita	A traditional Japanese response said at the completion of a meal, implying respect and appreciation. "It was very delicious."
Gomen nasai	pardon me, I apologize, forgive me
Gosei	fifth generation Japanese American
Haiseki	exclusion, prejudice
Haji	shame, disgrace on one's family or other Japanese
Hakujin	a white person, a Caucasian

Hapa	a mixed-race person, a term used in the U.S. among Japanese
Hina Matsuri	Girls' Day or Doll Festival celebrated on March 3.
Issei	a Japanese person who immigrated to and settled in the United States, a first generation Japanese American
Itadaki masu	A traditional and respectful phrase said before eating. It means, "I gratefully eat this meal you have prepared.
Itadake masho	A traditional and respectful phrase said before eating. It means, "Let's eat." or "Let us all partake."
It-te kimasu	I am going.
It-te irashai	Please be on your way.
Kami-sama	God, the creator
Kendo	a Japanese martial art using bamboo sticks for swords
Kibei	A Japanese American born in the U.S. who was educated as a child in Japan, and returned to the U.S.
Konnichi wa	Good day, good morning.
Mochi	a Japanese rice cake
Neh	"Isn't it?" or "Don't you think?"
Nisei	American-born, second-generation child of an *Issei*
Nikkei	a generic term applied to anyone Japanese
Ochitsuite yo	Be calm, self possessed.
Ohaiyo gozaimasu	Good morning.

Okaeri nasai	Welcome home.
Oya-koko	properly caring for one's parents beyond what is required
Oyasumi nasai	Good-night (when going to sleep).
On	a powerful sense of loyalty and respect for one's parents or teacher, moral obligation
San	an honorific form of address, used after a person's name or nickname
Sansei	third generation Japanese American, child of a *Nisei*
Senninbari	a thousand-stitch belt
Shamisen	a Japanese stringed instrument held like a guitar
Shikata ga nai	It cannot be helped.
Shikkari shite kudasai, neh	Be strong for all of us, all right?
Shikkari suru	Be strong, brave, steady.
Shinbo shimasho	Let us be patient, persevere, put up with.
Shoji panel	a sliding partition door made of a latticework wooden frame and covered with a tough, translucent white paper
Tabi	Japanese socks
Tadaima kaerimashita	I have just returned home.
Tango no Sekku	Boys' Day festival celebrated on May 5, later called Children's Day. Boy's day is also called *Kodomo no Hi.*
Umeboshi	sour plums
Wasabi	horseradish
Yonsei	fourth generation Japanese American

DISCUSSION QUESTIONS

1) What happened on the day Mary said her life changed forever? What changed for Mary on that particular day?

   At this point in your own life, have you experienced something that you feel has changed your life forever? If so, what happened?

2) Why is Mary conflicted about being Japanese and American? At what point did she start to feel this way?

   If you have a mixed cultural/racial background, do you feel conflicted? If so, what are the mixed feelings? If you do not come from a mixed background, what do you imagine would be things people from mixed backgrounds might be conflicted about?

3) Why did Mary and her family decide to burn their Japanese treasures?

   If you had been in Mary's situation, would you have burned your treasures? If so, what would you get rid of so the FBI wouldn't find it?

4) How many internment camps did Mary have to go to? Why did she move to different camps? What was the same and what was different about each camp?

5) When was the last time Mary danced a traditional Japanese dance? What happened and why did she decide to never dance again?

6) In Chapter 16 and Chapter 17, Mary writes about the huge conflict among Japanese Americans in the internment camps when filling out the questionnaire to determine their loyalty. Why did some people answer "Yes Yes" and others answered "No No"? Why did Mary decide to answer "Yes Yes"?

   If you had to decide for yourself, would you be a "Yes Yes" or a "No No" person? Why?

7) When Mary was having a difficult time living in the internment camps, Mama-san asked Mary to imagine twenty years
into the future, and look back at their experience in the internment camps. Mama-san suggested, "What kind of memories
do we want to have then of how we faced these difficulties
now." What did Mama-san mean when she said that? Was it
helpful to Mary?

*Can you think of something in your own life that is difficult that you
want to imagine looking back on twenty years from now? If so, how
would you like to remember it?*

8) Yoneichi never spoke much about his experiences fighting in
World War II.

*Why do you think he was reluctant to talk about it—not even telling
his family he had received a Bronze Medal?*

9) Why was Mary so emotionally torn and upset when she
read about the United States dropping an atomic bomb on
Hiroshima, Japan?

*If you were Mary's friend or classmate, what would you say to her
after hearing this news?*

10) Why did it take Mary so long to open up and tell the details
of her experiences in Japanese-American internment camps?
What were the cultural restrictions?

*Do you experience cultural restrictions in your own family? If so,
what are they? Would they keep you from sharing your own life
story?*

STUDENTS' WRITING AND RESEARCH ACTIVITIES

1) Imagine you have one week to pack two suitcases and prepare to leave your home. You can only take what you can carry. Remember, you don't know where you are going and what the weather will be like. You don't know how long you will be there or what you will be doing. Make a list of all the items you will take. Be sure to include eating utensils, personal toiletries, and sheets and towels.

   Next, see if all your items will fit in two small suitcases that you can carry. If you have pets, you must figure out who will take care of them because you cannot take them with you. You have one week to figure this out. Write out your plan.

2) Mary's parents came to the United States looking for a better life. Research and list at least five other groups of immigrants down through U.S. history who came to America looking for a better life. Include at least two groups of immigrants who are currenty coming to the U.S. seeking a better life.

   Interview someone you know who immigrated to the United States. Listen to his or her story and write it down. What have you learned from his or her experiences?

3) The title of this book, *Looking Like the Enemy*, is about being judged by the way you look, not by who you are. Write a personal story about how you have been judged by others because of the way you look. If you have not experienced this, find someone who has experienced prejudice because of their physical appearance, interview them, and write about their experiences.

4) Mary tells the story of imagining her favorite dessert—"the most luscious banana split"—when she only had one soda cracker to eat for a treat.

One night after dinner, skip dessert and instead, slowly eat one plain soda cracker. Close your eyes and imagine your favorite dessert. Write down the description in great detail, engaging as many of your senses as possible. You can also draw a detailed picture of this delicious treat.

5) World War II has been described as a "global military conflict." First, research and describe the two sides fighting in the War—the Allies and the Axis. Why were the Japanese-American soldiers so crucial in successfully defeating the Axis countries?

Second, research written stories of bravery by Japanese-American soldiers and share these with your class.

6) To this day, there is ongoing debate over the pros and cons of the United States dropping the first atomic bomb on Hiroshima, followed by a second atomic bomb dropped on Nagasaki, Japan. Research both sides, then share your opinions about this debate.

7) Today, Hiroshima, Japan is called "The City of Peace." In Peace Park, there are several memorials honoring those who died in the atomic bombing. One memorial is dedicated to a twelve-year-old girl, Sadako Sasaki, who was born after World War II, but suffered leukemia due to the atomic bomb. Read her story, *Sadako and the Thousand Paper Cranes.*

Learn how to make an origami paper crane. Research on the Internet to learn how to send your paper cranes to Peace Park and be placed at Sadako's memorial, along with tens-of-thousands of paper cranes made by people around the world.

8) On the Internet, research and "virtually visit" Japanese-American internment camps. Look at photographic collections and read other people's stories. Share your findings with family and friends.

ABOUT THE AUTHORS

Mary Matsuda Gruenewald's first book, her adult memoir, *Looking Like the Enemy*, (NewSage Press 2005) was published when she was 80 years old. Five years later, the Young Reader's edition of her memoir is now available. Mary hopes to reach as many people as possible with her important story about this difficult time in U.S. history and the mistreatment of Japanese Americans.

Mary speaks regularly about her experiences during World War II to a wide range of audiences, including grammar schools, high schools, colleges, and universities. Students nationwide use her book as a classroom text. Mary's story has also been featured in the National Geographic book, *Denied, Detained, Deported: Stories from the Dark Side of American Immigration,* by Ann Bausum.

Mary has written articles on the internment that have appeared in major newspapers, and she has presented radio commentaries for her local NPR station. In 2003, Mary received an Asian American Living Pioneer Award. Her adult memoir, *Looking Like the Enemy,* was nominated by the American Library Association in 2005 for its list of "Best Books for Young Adults."

Mary is presently working on a third book, sharing wisdom from her own life experiences and from her mother, Mama-san. She is a Registered Nurse and practiced nursing for more than twenty-five years. Mary lives in Seattle, and still visits her family farm on Vashon regularly.

Visit Mary's web site: www.lookingliketheenemy.com

Maureen R. Michelson has worked with Mary Matsuda Gruenewald as her editor and book publisher since 2004. She published Mary's memoir, *Looking Like the Enemy*, in 2005, and has been delighted with its wide and favorable acceptance by readers, libraries, and schools. Mary was interested in having her memoir reach a younger audience, so Maureen edited and adapted *Looking Like the Enemy* for young readers.

Maureen is the publisher of NewSage Press, which she founded in 1985. She is also the author of *Women & Work: Photographs and Personal Writings*, which the *New York Times Book Review* praised as "merging images of pioneer and role models into one—courageous, versatile, persistent human beings of whom society can be proud." This book was also chosen as a "Best Book for Young Adults" by the American Library Association. Maureen has written, edited and published books for more than 25 years. Prior to that, she was a journalist and worked for several publications, including *Time* and *People,* among others. Maureen lives and works in Portland, Oregon.

Visit NewSage Press's web site: www.newsagepress.com

OTHER BOOKS
BY NEWSAGE PRESS

One Woman One Vote: Rediscovering the Woman's Suffrage Movement
an anthology edited by Marjorie Spruill Wheeler

Jailed for Freedom: American Women Win the Vote
Doris Stevens, edited by Carol O'Hare

Organizing for Our Lives: New Voices from Rural Communities
Richard Steven Street and Samuel Orozco

Polar Dream: The First Solo Expedition by a Woman and Her Dog to the Magnetic North Pole
Helen Thayer

Whales: Touching the Mystery
Book and DVD by Doug Thompson, Foreword by Jane Goodall, Ph.D.

Singing to the Sound: Visions of Nature, Animals & Spirit
Brenda Peterson

Women & Work: In Their Own Words
edited by Maureen R. Michelson

*For a complete list of NewSage Press titles
visit our website: www.newsagepress.com,
or request a catalog from NewSage Press.*

NewSage Press
PO Box 607, Troutdale, OR 97060-0607

Phone Toll Free 877-695-2211
Email: info@newsagepress.com
Distributed to bookstores by Publishers Group West

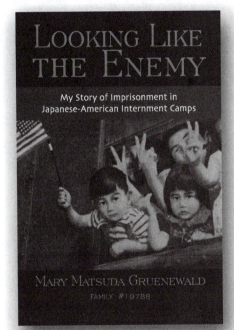